Endings That Begin...

Endings That Begin...

A Journey Into Love
Through The Universal Laws of Reciprocity

Ascyna Talking Raven,
Ricki Reynolds,
Marisol Dennis,
Naveen Varshneya,
Al Diaz,
Ashish Paul,
Jeni Lynn Allen

iUniverse LLC
Bloomington

Endings That Begin...
A Journey Into Love Through The Universal Laws of Reciprocity

iUniverse books may be ordered through booksellers or by contacting:

iUniverse LLC
1663 Liberty Drive
Bloomington, IN 47403
www.iuniverse.com
1-800-Authors (1-800-288-4677)

ISBN: 978-1-4759-4845-5 (sc)
ISBN: 978-1-4759-4846-2 (e)

Library of Congress Control Number: 2012916341

Printed in the United States of America.

iUniverse rev. date: 02/06/2014

This book is dedicated to

JON SEQUOIA ...
Who honors me by calling me his Beloved.

"If You want someone to follow you in a certain direction, the best way to do it is to make space for them to fall into."
~Jon Sequoia~

. . . And he has always made "space" for me to fall into . . .

. . . And my birth children
Beth
Tryn
Wynona
Donnette—who lives again in my inner village

. . . And to my children from another mother
Danny and **Kathy**

". . . . Universe at play inside your DNA, you are a billion years old today . . ."

~George Harrison from song: "The Rising Sun"~

"Everything you can imagine is real."

~Pablo Picasso~

Contents

Acknowledgments

My appreciation and gratitude to the many friends and family members who have walked me through the process of creating this book, and who blessed me with stories, letters and their very words that appear on these pages.

What an amazing journey the writing of this book has been. I never realized years ago when I began it, how many titles it would grow into, how much time it would take to bring it into birth, and how painful, and yet how joyful, that birth would be!

I am very full of gratitude to the many midwives who assisted in the birth, and to the village of friends who continued to share in the raising of it to maturity . . .

Special thanks and LOVE to Rev. Ricki Reynolds, Naveen Varshneya, Jeni Lynn Allen, Marisol Dennis, Dr. Ashish Paul, and Al Diaz, for their sharing of pages filled with the messages of love and hope given to them by the Creator, to share with all of us. Through our life stories and experiences shared on the pages of this book, our hope is that you will know love and Positive Abundance are yours for the Asking.

Last but not least, special thanks to Kirsten Laulainen, for editing this book. She has worked on a book for young adults, and a piece of visionary/speculative fiction, but this is her first book of this kind. Kirsten embodies love in all that she does, whether creating Oracle card decks, providing animal communication sessions, or editing spiritual/metaphysical fiction and nonfiction. The editing of this book was a unique experience, and in Kirsten's words, "This was the first time I really felt loved and lovable for giving my gift with language and words. I hope I can give the gift to all of you who read the words written here."

I have attempted to locate the author and copyright ownership of all quotes in this book; however, due to receiving them from so many sources, I have found I stand in a place of uncertainty as to where and to whom correct credit should go. I would greatly appreciate hearing from you if you know where proper credit may be given.

Preface

You already know what we are sharing with you. The Universal Laws of Reciprocity are a part of the very framework of our creation. These laws are the forces that create union, knowledge, power, connection and love. You have always known these laws; the knowledge of them came with you at your birth.

The Universal Laws of Reciprocity consist of five sub-laws. They are:

- Like Attracts Like
- What You Give Out Comes Back To You
- As You Believe, So Shall It Be
- What You Ask For, You Shall Receive
- The Collective Consciousness Lives In You

Living with and understanding these five laws is a journey into LOVE. Love of the Universe. Love of Mother-Father-God-Creator, The One Who Is. Love of our Earth. Love of All Our Relations. Love of Ourselves, and through the Love of Ourselves, Love of Our Ancestors.

We are sharing with you our remembering of these Laws, and how they came alive within us. Through living the teaching of these simple yet amazing Laws, we, the authors, have found LOVE, Abundance and Joy beyond our wildest dreams.

Our desire is to awaken within you the knowledge of the great gifts of power and creation found within The Universal Laws of Reciprocity.

Our wish is for you to find your own remembrances about how they have worked in your life, and continue to be a blessing or a curse. Hopefully our examples and stories will be the impetus to move you to more fully CHOOSE which path you will live by.

Our remembering triggers your remembering, and we both remember to remember.

A lot of remembering going on around here!

All of us have a destiny, like the outline of our life that came with us at birth. As we lived and walked our path of Growth and Learning, experiencing the dichotomies of our life, we filled in that outline with our story. Putting flesh on our own bones. One day, we stand filled full with life, young and old. We stand fulfilled and ready to follow the purpose(s) of our creation . . . walk the final pathway of our destiny—IF WE CHOOSE.

It is all about choosing.

Each choice takes us on a journey within our Destiny.

Each choice we make creates energy. Energy is a form of matter. The matter created with the use of energy is either full of light and is life enriching, or it is of a darker more negative energy. If it is negative, it fills our physical body with dark heavy bits of matter. The dark heavy energy gets stuck in the DNA of our cells.

Until one day, in some time, in some now, we choose to follow the higher path to enlightenment and awakening we mapped out for ourselves at the beginning of our time on this Earth, and free our body of this stuck and static energy matter. We accomplish this by thinking, moving, exploring, and allowing new and different patterns of growth and evolving to form in our life. Patterns that free the stuck-static energy from our cells, and our ancestors, and move us into a higher frequency of being.

In this state of being, We suddenly see we have been attracting into our life many things and people that are not for our highest good.

We change the belief systems that no longer serve us and are not ours.

We begin to understand that what we ask for truly does manifest in our life.

We realize that what we give out, either negative or positive, does come back to us.

We view the whole of humanity, our ancestors, and all living things in the Universe as a part of us.

This may sound strange to you, but somewhere in the course of our lives, We knew that the One Who Is would bring us together. There are, in our way of heart-thinking, no accidents. We, you, and us, created this moment in time to share the information in the following pages. We are thankful for you and the love you bring to us.

We do not ask you to agree with Us. Nor do we need for you to accept our truths found on these pages. They may not be your truths; however, in being drawn to read the words given to us that we now share with you, there may be something for you in them.

What I am thinking is who I AM today and tomorrow.

Message from Ascyna Talking Raven

This book has been many years in the writing. I have been on a huge learning curve, and have been blessed by people from all walks of life to grow into the work of DNA Re-Patterning. It all began in Spokane, Washington at a Body, Mind Spirit Expo where I listened to Margaret Ruby, founder of Possibilities DNA. She talked about DNA Re-Patterning and how it was a vehicle for clearing the body of trapped and static energy that created patterns of thought and action in our lives.

This is the DNA that gives us the emotional responses our ancestors experienced, stored in their DNA, and at our birth, became our DNA. We resurrect it in our body each time we experience an emotional response, and when we re-act to a moment of fear-or-love-filled emotion we have never experienced before that moment.

Fear-filled emotions of anger, vanity, greed, lust, and attachment are the ones that become trapped within our DNA and our very cells. Once we accept an emotion/reaction blindly as our own, it actually becomes implanted in our DNA as ours. It is anchored by the level and intensity of energy we bring forth at the height of our response. If it is not released from our physical cells, it can and does impact us on a physical, mental, emotional and spiritual level by becoming stuck in our tissues . . . our issues are truly in our tissues.

With a thought and the accompanying emotion, we are able to manifest joy or sadness, despondency or hope, spiritual freedom or slavery. A thought, such a small seemingly significant thing, and yet it is the creator of our lives.

The Universal Laws of Reciprocity is an invaluable set of rules for managing and creating the flow of our lives. By learning how to manage their effectiveness, we are able to rid our body of the trapped energy in our DNA memory banks.

You create your Life Puzzle
by taking pieces of truth, and cutting them
to fit into your own puzzle.

The Other Stories

**"One has not only an ability to perceive the
world, but an ability to alter one's perception
of it, more simply, one can change things by the
manner in which one looks at them."**
~Tony Robbins~

As I sit here, all these years later, I spend much time in contemplation with the "village that lives in my head." Village in your head? Yes, over the years of growth and learning, from being a very lonely child "creating" and "playing" with my imaginary friends, I began to imagine I was living in a village with them. They became my family and elders.

In this NOW, my village "houses" many of my ancestors, and loved ones who have guided me all my life. Always present, with a warm smile and words of encouragement, are my Romany Gypsy great grandmother, and her beloved, my great grand father, whom I call Grey Feather. He was a full-blooded Cherokee, who ended up carrying a Caucasian name to protect him and his children.

There is a hut at the outer part of the village that is the home of Little Deer, an amazing woman whom I have created to be an incarnation of me many lifetimes ago. There are too many to name here, and more people move into my village as my life continues to expand.

You see, what we imagine within our creative consciousness—with emotion—becomes a part of our reality, and is implanted within our DNA. Our stories—our very histories—are simply the truths about us that we create from our limited perspective and view of the world. A reality shared through us, from the histories of our ancestors, who are the

co-authors of our lives. ***We are the Collective Consciousness.***
We are always in the process of becoming the critical mass of consciousness, through the histories we are continually telling as: The Story of ME.

One evening, as I sat in contemplation around the fire of my village, I asked why I was unable to finish the books I had started writing many year ago.

Little Dear looked up from staring into the fire, smiled at me and said, "Through your words a handful of people will hear these messages. Through the words of many together, whole villages will be blessed by the messages. Share the pages of this book with other Way Showers and Light Workers."

I was thunderstruck! Of course! That was the answer! Share the book with other people who understand the Universal Laws of Reciprocity. Who have lived them, and learned how to use them to create a positive and abundant life for themselves. Immediately, names began to flow before my eyes, and the writer's block of years vanished.

**"The true sign of intelligence
is not knowledge, but imagination."**
~Albert Einstein~

Now within my village, and the reality of my outer world lives some beautiful BEings who have enriched all of our lives beyond measure, without our even knowing it.

**"Understand how special you are and the miracle
that you are, and so will everyone around you."**
~Al Diaz~

I "met" Al Diaz on Facebook. His energy and enthusiasm for life, and his message of Love totally enthralled me, because he knows, beyond a shadow of doubt, that he is LOVE, and just lets it flow out from inside himself to all the world.

Soon we had a friendship growing between us, and before I knew it, I was finishing this book, with him as one of the contributors, and honored to be a presenter September 22, 2012 in Tempe, Arizona a part of **"The Miracle of Love Tour 2012."** And when I called him to ask him to participate in this community project we are calling a book, he immediately said, "Like Attracts Like is Mine."

. . . And so it is.

Al Diaz, founder of Ilumine Ao, Keynote and International speaker, author of The Titus Concept and Confirmations, cutting-edge internet radio show host, and Guide who has inspired thousands with his empowering message of Unconditional Love to simply shatter that which no longer stands to serve for our best and highest good. Al speaks from the Heart with his guidance and insights for us to remember our own answers that we are seeking and that allows us to see and feel the "Truth" that is already within all of us. In doing so, this raises our level of awareness and brings forth the consciousness for healing, blessings, and empowerment, triggering shift and change, ascension through Love, discovering newer dimensions that represent liberation, and the freeing of our Heart for our own personal greatness.

www.ilumine-ao.com

Tour website: www.themiracleoflove.com

But that is just part of the story . . .

> **"My Nana, so wise and full of advice,**
> **once said to me, 'If you are going to be thinking,**
> **better think about good things, otherwise**
> **you will meet lots of bad things.'"**
> ~Jeni Lynn Allen~

Through Al, I "met" Jeni Lynn Allen. I subscribed to her on Facebook, and began reading her posts. Posts full of optimism and positive abundance, JOY and LOVE. When I would sit in council in the village, her name kept popping into my head to be one of this book's contributors. I asked. She accepted.

Not the end of the story, but another beginning.

Jeni Lynn Allen was born and raised in the suburbs of Los Angeles, CA. Her life's work is dedicated to supporting individuals who are in pursuit of their dreams. As a Publicist and Marketing Specialist at Omni One Media, which services the entertainment, literature, entrepreneur and small business sectors, she has the opportunity to lift up others to accomplish their goals in their natural talents. And by doing so she is fulfilling her own dreams.

Jeni also enjoys public speaking, offering insights on various areas of life. She is committed to healing family bonds through therapeutic discoveries such as Family Grief Support and Art Therapy. Jeni is trained in family support with the Arnold C Yoder Foundation. She is a 'Universal Thinker' and believes and speaks on the need for Unconditional Love in our lives, the importance of forgiveness and also bringing awareness to young parents about their child's natural talents and how to nurture them.

~*~

". . . Everything in the universe is vibrating, nothing is fixed. So is death and destiny."
~Naveen Varshneya~

Ah, Facebook. So maligned and misunderstood by many, and yet such an awesome contribution to my world. Through this social media, I "met" Naveen Varshneya. For years I had been drawn to India. Was fascinated by it, and loved the teaching of its spiritual leaders. Naveen and I connected on a soul level like old friends meeting for the first time after years apart. I asked him to contribute a chapter on one of the laws. He accepted, and shortly after began a whole new and awesome chapter in his own life. I look forward to the time when I can meet, in the flesh so to speak, with this evolving being and his family.

Naveen Varshneya lives in India and is the discoverer of a protocol to reverse mental disorder. He established the theory and science of mental disorder, its causes and cure. He states, "Every problem carries seeds of its solution. Every disorder is a path wrongly chosen at the energetic level. To cure, just reverse the path at the spirit-mind-body level." At 42 he "hung up his boots" as a serial entrepreneur when he realized he was too ahead of his time, and resources were too limited to make evolutionary impact in the world. He lives and travels around the world inventing technologies and solution for social reforms.

~*~

"We are not just our bodies or our minds, but mind-body-spirit, and they work in relation to each other."
~Ashish Paul~

And again through the blessings of social media, I "met" Ashish Paul. This wise women of medicine, (or is it this wise medicine women?) has blessed so many lives with her wisdom, laughter and unconditional love. And with that unconditional love and quest for the ANSWERS OF LIFE, Ashish brings her fresh and inspiring "voice" to the pages of this writing.

Dr. Ashish Paul is a doctor of Ayurvedic and Western Herbal Medicine, focusing on Organic and Vegetarian protocols. She is passionate about educating and raising the awareness about Ayurveda to the public as well as professionals. Ashish lives in the UK with her twins, and can be reached through her website: www.ayuva.com

~*~

"Some creations take time and work, others transcend time and are instantaneous. Manifestations can be changed right down to our DNA."
~Ricki Reynolds~

Years ago, I was a student at The Northwest School of Religious and Philosophical Studies, and met Ricki Reynolds. Bright and Cheerful, full of Enthusiasm, and working toward awakening right along with the rest of us. What a great feeling it was to find myself in a room with people who were mortal, but all vibrating in a compatible frequency with me.

Ricki and I definitely had a connection that came from an earlier time in our being. When I contacted her to be one of the contributors, she humbly accepted and began to walk the walk of filling pages with her knowingness to share with us.

Ricki Reynolds was raised in the Southwest, and grew up with the love of people, nature, and animals. Ricki studied Ministry at the Northwest School for Religious and Philosophical Studies in Coeur d' Alene Idaho, under the mentorship of Marian Breckenridge and Lee Thompson, and was ordained in 2007. Ricki has studied a variety of healing modalities including Pranic Healing, EFT (Emotional Freedom Technique), and Matrix work, and conducts workshops in Inner Child Healing and Prayer Therapy. Ricki uses her Ordination for animal blessings. She works as an educator in the Allied Health Field, and has an AS degree in Medical Office Management.

~*~

**"I believe in the power of the human spirit.
I believe that once we break out of the chains that
hold us back we will uncover our greatness and
change the whole world. Stick it out, don't quit,
and before you know it, you are growing
by leaps and bounds."**
~Marisol Dennis~

Marisol is an amazing woman who fought a battle with a common enemy many of us are all too familiar with: cancer. But through the power of her faith, became the victor. The growth of knowing that came to her, just had to be shared with the rest of us. Her story, although somewhat commonplace, carries with it a unique and powerful twist of Love and confidence that is an inspiration to me. "If I, who am the least of these my brothers and sisters, KNOW that if I ask, it shall be given unto me . . . and I AM healed"

We too became acquainted through Facebook, and energetically through the magic that we take so for granted in this world, ENERGY exchange—even over long distance—she and I became friends.

Marisol Dennis is a single Mother of 4 wonderful children and Grandmother of 3 awesome Grandchildren. She is a graduate of Stockton State College, with a Bachelor of Science in Info Systems and Programming. Marisol is the Founder and CEO of Urban Computer Academy. She is a Cancer survivor and home based business entrepreneur.

Visit her website: http://marisoldennis.com/about_me
Visit her blog: http://www.empowernetwork.com/marisoldennis/blog/who-is-marisol-dennis/?id=marisoldennis

**"We have before us the glorious opportunity
to inject a new dimension of love into the veins
of our civilization."**
~Martin Luther King~

Chapter 1

The Journey Of ONE

**"Gifts to become one with each other
Thinking, persistence, listening, learning,
sharing, caring."**
~Louise Hayes~

There comes a time within the collective consciousness, that a critical mass is reached. When this occurs, it is as if everyone is suddenly aware of knowing something that they had not known before. I feel that this is what happened to me with this information. Why the One Who Is chose me to bring it into this reality is another story.

When I was 38 years old, I was given a death sentence from a very kind, compassionate doctor. He was young, just beginning his practice the day I was brought into his office. Tests were run, liver cancer the dreaded news. This blessed man is a Naturopath/Homeopath, so we tried everything known in alternative medicine to no avail. My life continued to flow out of the body, as I grew weaker and weaker.

I read a book by Dr. Bernie Siegel, <u>Love, Medicine and Miracles</u>. I learned about visualization and how it can affect disease. Read about *prayer and grew to know it is another form of visualization.* I prayed day and night. I used my imagination to visualize the disease as black gunk on my liver and saw little scrubbing bubbles scooping it away and removing it from my body, still the disease progressed. What was wrong? Why did this stuff work for others and not me? Was this my time to die? Then came the visit to the doctor where I was given the

Death Sentence. And I was mad! Six months! I had to wait six more months before I could leave this misery my life had become?! How unfair and cruel!

During the course of my illness, I had been experiencing very high fevers—106°F. Sometime for days, I would be swept away in a fever hallucination full of bears in my bedroom and vivid dreaming about falling into the sun. Nothing brought them down lower than 104°F, and it stayed at 106°F for days at a time. My body was wracked with pain so deep that it went beyond feeling. I knew I was dying.

Here's where I get to tell you about the bear. Many people wanted to help me, but didn't know how. Serious debilitating illness creates a deep sense of helplessness in people, and they become uncomfortable not knowing what to do to help the sick person. One couple, Bill and Jane Johnson, [not their real names], decided that I needed a good home-cooked meal and the siding put on my house—and a little companion—a dachshund named Sassy. To them, this was a gift of nourishment, and the best way they could share their healing energy with me.

On a beautiful day in late September, they came over to gift me with their service of love. Bill had killed a bear and Jane decided to cook a bear roast with mashed potatoes, gravy, corn and salad. The smell of the meat cooking was hard on my stomach, but I could not offend these two blessed people. I figured I would take a bite or two and stir the rest around on my plate, claiming lack of appetite. This was true; I hadn't had an appetite for weeks, and was on a macro-biotic diet.

Bill hammered away, Jane hummed in my kitchen preparing "the feast," and I lay in bed drifting in and out of a fevered sleep. I am enjoying the day. Not many more days on this earth for me to enjoy. There is much I will miss of this planet when I am on the "other side": the sky; brilliant sunlight and starry nights; cloudy days with rain and thunder; the smile on the faces of my children on Christmas morning—the list is so long that it would fill a book.

Jane climbed the stairs with my plate of food, propped me up in bed and placed the plate on my bed tray. There I am, starring at a plate full of meat and potatoes, and hoping I can get a couple of bites to reach my stomach and stay there. The salad looks safe, a couple of bites of it should be okay, but the meat . . . don't know if I can keep even one itty-bitty bite in my mouth.

Suddenly, in the corner of the room, beside my dresser, there was a bear! He is sitting on his haunches just staring at me with big sad eyes. I stabbed a piece of meat onto my fork and brought it to my mouth; he rose up as if to stop me. I put the fork back in my plate; he sat back down. This up and down thing went on for about 30 seconds before I said, "I don't want to eat you anyway," and gave the plate to the dogs. The bear disappeared. Wow! What an imagination I had! The things you see in a fever!

Friends came in and out of the house caring for me, but most of the day I was alone, just looking out of my bedroom window at a huge cottonwood tree as it changed colors. Summer rushed away, Fall was settling in with all the changes of beautiful color it carried. I prepared to die. Then as quickly as one blink of an eye, my life changed.

It was early morning and I had slept restlessly the night before, couldn't think about eating anything, and beginning to suffer from the effects of dehydration. I was dozing with a light breeze from the open window flowing across my fever-ravaged body. I was covered with a sheet and wearing a light cotton gown. I suddenly sensed someone looking at me. Fear grabbed me by the throat. I hoped it wasn't the bear again. Peeking out from between my eyelashes, I saw a strikingly handsome man at the foot of my bed. *Well,* I thought, *at least my hallucinations are getting better!*

He was robed in soft white that shimmered with the breeze from the open window. The kindest aquamarine eyes I had ever seen peered at me from a face of remarkable love. Dark brown hair gently surrounded his head and he stood somewhere close to six feet tall. He raised his hands toward me and with a beseeching gesture of his hands said, "It is time to depart this vessel and return to the One Who Is. Your vessel is beyond restoration. I have been sent to escort you." I just knew it was my wishful thinking speaking to me at the foot of my bed. Wait till I tell my friends about this one!

He began to chant strange and eerie words in a monotone sing song tone. I felt like the hair on my head was standing straight up, as the room became charged with static electricity. A sense of euphoria crept from my toes to the top of my head. I felt like I was being dissolved and pulled toward his hands.

At this point, as I began to feel like I was turning to liquid. Beside the bed next to me appeared another gorgeous man. This being was about the same height as the one at the foot of the bed, but his hair was a light brown and his eyes were a bluer shade of color. He held up his hand toward the man at the foot of the bed and said, "Halt! She is not to leave this incarnation yet. There is much work for her to finish, that she covenanted to do in this incarnation."

As I lay there, thinking that things were getting pretty weird in my bedroom, the being at the foot of my bed said, "By whose authority do you require me to stop extracting this soul?"

"By the authority of (this name still remains unheard in my head), who has charge of this one's current incarnation." I was very absorbed in what this being was saying, and trying to understand the name he had mentioned. It was as if they were speaking in a foreign language, and yet I knew what they were saying, but couldn't make out the name of authority.

"I bow to His authority and commands," said the dark haired being, and when I looked to the foot of my bed, he was gone.

Whew! This hallucinating stuff is tiring! So thinking, I began to drift off to sleep. Drifting was as far as I got before the voice of the being beside me reminded me that he was still there.

"I have been sent to repair and restore the vessel with which you clothe yourself, that you may be able to continue in this incarnation, and fulfill the covenants you made."

This was confusing to me, as the handsome being at the foot of my bed had stated quite emphatically that my 'vessel' was beyond repair. While I was pondering over this inconsistency in my hallucination, and thinking it didn't matter, because it was all my fever-induced imagination anyway, it did not occur to me that I should question him about my confusion. After all, he was just a product of my fever.

The being beside me continued his instructions. "When I have completed this task, you will release body fluid from every orifice and pore of your physical body. This substance will be very toxic to any living being from this dimension. Next, you will wash your body to remove the residue. When the cleansing is complete, you will gather up all the soiled bedding, and receptacles of fluid waste, and put it all in a deep hole for the Earth to take care of. After placing it in the Earth, you will burn off as much as will allow itself to be consumed in fire, and then fill the soil of the Earth over it."

Right! I thought. *I can hardly get out of bed to use the bedside commode!* That's why we had put an old plastic shower curtain under the sheet, so I wouldn't soil the mattress. *But* according to this being, I was going to wash myself, gather everything up, and take it down the stairs, down the hillside to level ground, dig a hole, throw it in, set it on fire, and then top it off by tossing dirt in the hole! Now I knew I was having a really whopper of a hallucination!

So thinking, I began to drift off to sleep. My eyes were suddenly jerked open when high-pitched sounds began to fill the room. He had his hands about six inches from my body and was moving them in a rhythmic back and forth motion from my head to my feet. From his mouth were sounding tones that I didn't think could be made on this Earth. They weren't unpleasant, but very strange to my uneducated ears. Without knowing it at the time, I was receiving an energy treatment of celestial proportions. This time when my eyes closed, I did sleep.

Sometime later, I awoke to find him gone. Well, at least I hadn't been bored this day. No sooner had that thought rushed through my mind, then I began to sweat, and barely made it to the bedside commode before I began to release from my body an amazing amount of matter. I grabbed a large bowl from beside the bed and hung my head over it. From my eyes, nose, ears and mouth more "stuff" flowed. Oily sweat rolled off my body. It smelled terrible. I could hardly breathe. Just as quickly as it began, it stopped.

The only thing I could think was, *this can't be real.* But it was real. I thought I had better do what the Being said, so I walked to the middle of the room and standing on another shower curtain we had placed on the floor for bathing purposes, poured water on a cloth, and began to wash my body, adding more water to remove the residue of sweat and then rinse my body.

Where was the energy coming from for me to complete this task? Amazement began to fill my heart when I realized that the fever was gone! Six weeks of misery were over. And I was infused with new energy, still weak, but at least able to walk.

I began to gather everything as instructed by the "hallucination," and walked down the stairs for the first time in two months. Dressed in the clothes in which I was born, I grabbed some matches on the way out the door. Looking down the hillside, I noticed a huge hole in the Earth. *At least I won't have to dig a hole*, I thought. There was the unfilled perk test hole for a septic system made before I took to my bed. No one had bothered to fill it.

With the relief of knowing my task would not be so difficult, I walked down the hillside to the hole in the earth. Right beside the test hole was a pile of wood that hadn't been cut into firewood, and a can of saw gas! This was getting better and better! I tossed in the huge Santa Claus bundle of "goodies" and poured gas over it, flicked a lit match into the hole, and watched it burn for a couple of minutes. I grabbed the shovel, so conveniently left by the hole, tossed in a few shovelfuls of dirt, and dragged myself up the hill. I walked naked into the house and up the stairs, threw the blanket at the foot of the bed over the mattress, and collapsed into a deep, restful sleep for the first time in weeks.

"I am not my thoughts, emotions, sense of perceptions, and experiences. I am not the content of my life. I am life, I am the space in which all things happen. I am consciousness, I am the Now."
~Eckhart Tolle~

Now, if I had just read this story, I would wonder why it was in the beginning of a book about living The Universal Laws of Reciprocity. It is here, because it is how I was prepared to live, to share it with you today, as an example of how this law works in our lives.

Did it really happen? Was it just a whopper of a hallucination that I was able to manifest, because I wanted to live? You tell me.

"We think we understand the rules when we become adults, but what we really experience is a narrowing of the imagination."
~David Lynch~

Many of us, when we were children we had imaginary friends. To us they were very real. They comforted us, played with us and taught us. Some of us never believed the grown-ups when they told us our friends weren't real. I continued to talk and play with mine in secret, just like many other children did. I like to think, as I heard in a movie the other day, that God is the imaginary friend of adults. This makes so much sense to me, since I have had "imaginary" celestial beings as my friends for all my life.

You must use your imagination, and allow the possibility of this story of mine being real to bring it into your understanding. I can't explain how it works; I just know it does.

"YOU are here to enable the Divine Purpose of the Universe to unfold . . . THAT is HOW IMPORTANT YOU ARE!"
~Echart Tolle~

Chapter 2

Consider This

"The intellect has little to do on the road to discovery. There comes a leap in Consciousness, call it intuition or what you will, and the solution comes to you and you don't know how or why."
~Albert Einstein~

For the course of this sharing, I ask you to put aside any other teaching you have followed about The Universal Laws . . . and

Just for the next few minutes . . .

Consider That:

- You are a multidimensional being, with all of "time" in this NOW.

I am a joyous and creative expression of the One Who Is.

- All the beings that are connected to you through your blood-line DNA are with you in this *Now*.

- It is necessary to develop a daily spiritual practice that encourages you to pay attention to how you spend your energy each day. Do you invest your energy in the false emotion of fear or in the true emotion of love?

- You have a vast database of stored information and experiences called DNA/RNA. This information, and the experiences that are stored within it, is encoded and stored in one of the energy centers of your physical body called Chakras, and in your organs—especially your heart, brain and glands. Each of your Chakras stores information and experiences that are specific to the area of your body associated with it. Example: Solar Plexus Chakras (liver) records and stores unprocessed anger and frustration; Sex Chakra/ Root Chakras/ Base Chakra (kidney, pelvic region) records and stores fear and loss of power.

- Developing a daily Spiritual practice gives you the understanding of how to listen to your bodies and determine how you are using, and storing information as energy in of each Chakra center.

- It is important to always remember you loose or give away your power of life when you focus on fears and expectations, and create a future that you and your descendants will not like. **What you focus on becomes your reality**.

- The majority of recorded and stored information and experiences came to you, and with you, at your birth. It is in the DNA of your family bloodline. It is as eternal and celestial as the very Universe in which our Earth lives.

- All the powerful teachings—for GOOD or BAD—(these are used here as a frame of reference, not as a concept), are readily available for you to use in your life at ALL TIMES—past and present and future—and these teachings are available to you in this NOW.

- **We are Energy beings.** DNA is a stored form of energy. Your thoughts are energy. Scientists have found that energy is matter. It is a finite form of matter, and can be manipulated just like all matter. All forms of energy has it's own vibrational signature of frequency.

- Your **breath connects with your thoughts through the power of sound**, through the words you speak, and those thoughts are anchored in your DNA by your emotions, the words you speak, and your actions.

- **Fear is an emotion that comes to you from the past through your DNA.** It is known as *Fight or Flight*. Even though most of your DNA comes to you at your birth, during this incarnation, you add your imprints based on how you react to your situation, and attach an associated memory from your DNA stored memories. Remember, **like attracts like. You are the collective consciousness . . . it lives inside your very cells . . .**

- Your ancestors' memories are stored in your DNA, and you carry it around within your cells. This "baggage" is not yours and does not serve you in your life. In order for you to be truly connected with your life, and become fully aware and awake, this dense and "stuck" energy must be cleared from your physical and emotional bodies.

- When you have restored equanimity to your bodies, harmony with your environment is in place, and "you" exist without the "baggage" of your bloodline. This allows you to encode on a conscious level and awaken to the life you were meant to live by the One Who Is.

- Your hands move energy within and around your body, connecting the lower half with the upper half of your body, and encouraging your body to discharge "stuck" energy and anchoring healing/balancing energy on a cellular level.

- Your head-brain (mind) lives in fear of loosing its hold on the physical body, and it fears loosing its conscious state of control, and end its existence. Connect with your mind that is centered in the brain. It is the creative processor of your being. Love your mind, and make it a vital part of you.

What I think today blesses my tomorrow.

- How you feel about yourself determines how your mind will react to your day, and what will be recorded and stored in your database for future carriers of your DNA to experience. **Your choices create the life you will live one day at a time in this NOW, and ripple down the time-line, back and forward creating life for those connected to you through your DNA.**

- Creation and Manifestation are 50% intention and 50% imagination. **All great beginnings started with *intention* and *imagination*.**

- **Your *imagination* is the most powerful creative tool you will ever possess.**

- Many benefits come to you by preparing your mind to enter your day feeling good (love), and not continuing to live in the shadow side of life called illusion and created by fear.

- Your physical body has its own natural wisdom, and at all times works with your heart to allow the natural life giving energy from the One Who Is to flow freely to you.

My creative source is always available to me.

- There is a "Collective Mind" that influences the way you think. If you are still thinking with your demanding brain and not your loving heart-brain, your choices are most often influenced by the fear-based emotions and your life may be more challenging than you desire.

What I think and feel with my heart-centered-brain creates my tomorrow.

- When you become separated from, or closed off from, your heart center, you will not be able to know you are loved, and fear becomes your primary emotion: fear of lack, fear of not being good enough, fear of being rejected, ridiculed, etc.

I am making positive changes in my life.

- You are 100% responsible for your wellness, well-being and happiness by the way you respond to the stimulus from the people and situations in your life. By your choices and perceptions, your world is created and your future prepared. You have total control over your external world. Remind yourself that you are sharing love or fear with everyone you meet! Stand in the light of love, and the shadow of fear will begin to dissipate.

- Caroline Myss states in her <u>Chakra Meditation Music,</u> "Forgiveness is not easy, but today I ask for one more step toward that goal." *Forgiveness is the medicine of this new century, and energy medicines; like DNA Re-Patterning, Pranic Healing, Reiki, EFT, and a multitude of others, are the pathway to it.*

"Anytime you start a sentence with I am, you are creating what you are and what you want to be . . ."
~Dr. Wayne Dyer~

- Words we use to react and act within our world greatly impact our bodies. **Words are vibrations, and have a frequency.** These vibrations carried by our intentions for speaking them, implant within the cells of our bodies, into our very DNA. When these words are spoken with anger, or any form of fear present **within** us, they are like dull, double-edged swords thrust into our body and BEcome stuck.

"Everything we call real is made of things that cannot be regarded as real."
~Niels Bohr~
Nobel-Prize-winning physicist

Chapter 3

The Hundredth Monkey Revisited

**"When a certain number of people come together,
and they choose at a moment in time to create
a precise emotion in their hearts, that emotion
literally can intentionally influence the very fields
that sustain life on planet Earth."**
~ Gregg Braden~

There is an urban legend that is a great example for me to share the Law of Reciprocity with you . . . maybe you have read it or heard it before, but never like I will share it with you!

During the 1950's there was quite a controversy going on in the world. It was between the Creationist and the Evolutionist, and was started by Darwin when he wrote <u>On The Origin of Species.</u> The scientists of the world were determined to prove that hu-mans evolved from primates. The Japanese sent teams of scientists and animal behaviorist to study the troops of monkeys on several islands in the South Pacific. The study was to establish proof that the primates functioned in a society similar to hu-mans, and thus conclusively show they are a part of the same evolutionary path.

On the islands the teams observed the monkeys from blinds they had built away from the beach and in the tree line. They observed these delightful animals as they hung out on or around the beach. The monkeys loved to frolic in the sand, and interacted in very similar ways with each other as their human counterparts do . . . but they didn't build sand castles. **(Like Attracts Like)**

The teams knew that the monkeys loved sweet potatoes, and would toss pieces of them onto the beach. This gave them an opportunity to observe more closely, in a controlled study, how the monkeys interacted with each other . . . but the monkeys hated the sand that coated the pieces of sweet potato. They would rub them on their hair, try to brush it off, and eat the pieces with a grimace.

On one particular island, when the monkeys had "soiled" one portion of the beach, they would move to the next section. As they worked and played their way around the island, they seemed to know that the ocean tides would "clean" the shore. The teams of scientists were excited about this, because it showed a thinking process similar to indigenous hu-mans.

One day, the troop of monkeys moved to a portion of the beach that was intersected by a stream flowing to the ocean. Magically the pieces of detectible food fell from the sky, thrown by the "Gods" and of course, just like it had always been, the sand was all over them. Little monkeys complained to their parents about the sand. Older monkeys complained to the elders about the sand, but the elders seemed say "This was the way the 'Gods' intended for us to have the treats. We must accept them as they are given to us." **(As You Believe, So Shall It BE)**

One of the more "enlightened" monkeys, whom we will fondly name Betty, deciding she did not want to squabble on the beach for her morning treat, had wandered close to a stream that intersected the beach and flowed into the ocean. Lo and behold, she spied a few of the detectible treats from the "Gods" in the water of the stream.

Checking to see if anyone else had noticed this bounty, she quickly reached into the water, grabbed a piece, and promptly plopped it into her mouth. Something was missing.

She quickly realized there wasn't any sand on it! *Well, maybe this was just a fluke,* she thought. *After all, there has always been sand on these treats.* She reached into the water, scooped up another piece of sweet potato, and tentatively plopped it into her mouth. Wow! Still no sand. Now she was excited!

She surreptitiously strolled over to her friend Martha, (another enlightened Being), and quietly said, "Martha come with me. I have a surprise for you. Don't eat that sandy treat; bring it with you. Don't dawdle. Bring it with you."

The two of them strolled casually to the stream. Upon reaching it, Betty said to Martha, "Do you see the pieces of treat in the water? Pick one up, and put it in your mouth."

Martha picked one up, and started to wipe the sand off, but Betty told her to just put it in her mouth. Martha grimaced as she slowly placed the treat in her mouth, and began to chew. She realized quickly there was no sand on it! Eyes wide open, she turned to her friend and asked, "Betty, how can this be? There has always been sand on the treats from the 'Gods.' No matter how much we wished there was no sand on them, it has always been there. I am afraid! Maybe this is an evil thing!"

(What You Ask for You SHALL Receive)

Betty, the First Monkey shakes her head and said, "How can something that we have asked for many times be evil? I think it is the water that has washed the sand off the treats. Take your piece from the beach, and swish it around in the water.

Martha opened her hand, and eyed the sandy treat in it, swished it around in the water of the stream, and tentatively placed it in her mouth. With eyes wide again, she said, "The water removes the sand! It has to be magic! Let's go tell everyone about this miracle!"

The two friends rushed onto the beach to share this exciting discovery. As you can imagine their discovery was met with skepticism and derision. "After all," the elder monkeys said, "This is how the 'Gods' gave it to us, and if they wanted it to be sand-free, they would have given it to us sand-free!"

This rejection did not deter our pair of crusaders, they talked to every monkey they met, teaching them how to wash the sand off their sweet potato treats. One by one the monkeys in the troop on this island began to wash the sand off their treats, and share their excitement with their friends and family. **(What You Give Out Comes Back to You)**

When the 99th monkey was convinced to wash her treats, and taught the 100th monkey to wash their treat in the ocean or a stream, the Japanese scientists were amazed by what happened, the next morning after they threw out the sweet potato pieces!

That fateful morning, *every monkey* on the island automatically, as if they had been doing it every day, picked up their treats, walked to the water, and washed the sand off before eating them. The most amazing part of this event was yet to be revealed. The reports started coming in from the other island's scientific teams. *All* the monkeys on *all* the islands had picked up their treats, taken them to the water, and washed off the sand! **(Critical Mass Consciousness BEcomes)**

AND . . .

The Hundredth-Monkey Phenomenon happened!

The Power of The Universal Laws of Reciprocity is manifest.

". . . An innate ability and thinking process occurred, and the collective thought process created a Critical Mass within us, and it becomes a new trait within the species."
~Lyle Watson~

Chapter 4

The 12 Universal Laws
By: Christin Sanders

"Universal Laws Cannot NOT Happen."
~Saundra Pathweaver~

Many people are familiar with the "Law of Attraction" now due to the popularity of the book and movie The Secret. Unfortunately the laws of the universe are a bit more complicated than all that. Although movies like this are a great primer for introducing people to universal laws, they fall a bit short in their ability to teach people all they need to know. Due to its limited size, it over-simplified a lot of things that I feel are very important to understanding and working with the Universal laws in meaningful ways.

Many people get frustrated with trying to manifest their ideal reality. They try things like vision boards, affirmations, focusing on what they do want etc. only to find that they are still coming up short. They may target this energy to things like money or cars, when what they truly want is security and freedom. Does the law of attraction even work? Yes. Yes it does, but it requires a deeper understanding and application of all of the universal laws together in order to truly make it work in your life.

You see, the law of attraction is merely one of the twelve—yes twelve—universal laws. Recognizing and getting a brief understanding of the full circle of universal laws will make working with the "Law of Attraction" easier. Trying to work with only the Law of Attraction is like trying to catch a fish without a hook, or bait, or the fishing pole. You could just hop in the water and try to grab the fish, but it sure is easier when you have a tool and know how to work with all of its respective, but interconnected parts.

So, here are the other universal laws explained in a nutshell with some real-life examples. More searching and seeking is recommended—but hopefully this will spark the desire to learn more.

The Law of Divine Oneness

There is one word I love that I believe sums this law up nicely—Namaste.

In it's literal translation "I bow to you" what it truly means is: I honor the place in you where the light of God abides—when I am in that place in me and you are in that place in you—there is one of us. In other words, all things are connected and we are all one. It is a way of acknowledging and recognizing that connection we all share.

All life, all energy comes from one source. We are all connected—period. It doesn't merely extend to those we deem likeable or those who believe what we do etc. We all come from the same source and are living expressions of the divine. We must learn to recognize the divinity that is within all things and respect it.

You are not a tiny, insignificant drop in a vast ocean. Your goal is to learn to see the ocean within the drop. Those who see themselves as perpetually "small" are sending vibrational energies that are also "small." You are a part of an energy source that is so vast, so immeasurable that the mind cannot comprehend it. This lies at the core of you—and every being.

The Law of Vibration

This law states that all things are made of energy.

You've like heard the phrase "vibes" as in "I didn't like that place it had a weird vibe." We are able to intuitively sense the energies around objects, places, other people etc. The Law of Vibration tells us we must align our energy with what we want to attract. We do this through the power of our emotions (as a sort of barometer to tell us if we are on the right path) and our thoughts, which we can choose to redirect at any moment. Feelings and thoughts combined are powerful things.

A good lesson here is learn to let go! If something irritates you, bless it for teaching you a lesson in spiritual wisdom and then send it packing. :) Not fully recognizing this Law is also why the Law of Attraction fails miserably for many people. You must truly act as if you are already what you WANT to be, in order to align your energy with that and help it manifest. Notice I said, "help." Keep reading ;)

The Law of Action

This rule states that you must facilitate the other laws with inspired action.

You cannot sit on your butt and expect things to fall into your lap without effort. Does this mean you have to struggle? Absolutely not! If you are "struggling" to reach your goals it means you are not aligned with them properly, or that they are not the right goals for you.

Hard work, when it is something you are passionate about, should be challenging, but also come easy. For me, it's writing. I know that my writing flows easily because it is what I love, and it is the tool that allows me to do what I am most passionate about—helping others. I also challenge myself to write in different ways and to try new things in life so I have more to write about! You must take inspired actions every day that help you move towards your goals. Without action, you might as well forget the rest.

The Law of Correspondence

This law states that your outer world reflects your inner world.

Simply stated, you are destined to experience what you think about and your world reflects this to you every day. If you want to change external circumstances in your life, you must change your inner world first.

Those who seek inner peace and clarity find that their daily lives and routines flow more easily and harmoniously. They are better able to cope with life's little upheavals and carry on. Those who get stuck in anger, resentment, and other self-sabotaging emotions and beliefs find that they tend to draw more chaos into their lives—and they likely don't realize they are doing it.

For example, I turn the TV OFF. I read just enough news once or twice a week to stay abreast of what is going on. As a society we tend to focus on the negative. News broadcasts bombard us with hundreds of negative thoughts, images, etc. In turn, our society has become paranoid and fear fuels so many things. When I was a kid, I ran around outside until it was dark. Today kids are stuck inside because everyone is terrified of the bogeyman. We have a skewed perception of how the world actually is because we feed that image regularly. I refuse to live life according to fear. Want to see how beautiful the world is? Go outside on a sunny day and smile at a stranger. Chances are they aren't going to mug or kill you—they'll probably smile back.

The Law of Cause and Effect

This law states that what you do comes back to you.

Many spiritual traditions have taught this universal wisdom in various ways. The most well known, "You reap what you sow" or "karma." If you are passionate and driven in positive ways, you will put forth powerful energy and actions that will return to you in the form of rewards. On the other hand, if you are negative and hurtful towards yourself and others, this returns to you as well in the form of consequences.

The Law of Attraction

Like attracts like. Positive energies will attract more positive energies and vice versa.

This is why it is important to focus on manifesting positive energy through the use of the various laws of the universe. It goes beyond merely "wishing" or "hoping" or "visualizing" as so many others teach. If you want to attract positive energy—you have to line up with it and apply yourself.

The Law of Compensation

You get back what you give to others.

There is a saying "misery loves company." It means that when you are miserable, you tend to attract other people who are also miserable and it becomes a vicious circle that sort of feeds on itself.

Fortunately, the opposite is true—if you want to receive more of something in your life—be what you want to see! Give freely to others what you hope to receive. Does this mean if you need more money you should throw away the money you do have? No, but you should be generous and share abundance according to your current capacity to do so.

Provide for those who are in need by giving of yourself. Be generous and share abundance in its many forms with others—and abundance and prosperity will return to you.

The Law of Perpetual Transmutation of Energy

Energy is in constant motion and all energy eventually manifests.

This Law also states that you have the power to change your life—higher vibrational energies consume lower energies—so if you don't like the path you are on—change it, or more importantly "allow" it to be changed.

Rather than try to "force your will" on people or circumstances, rearrange the way you think and choose to empower yourself. I call this The Learning-To-Go-With-The-Flow Law. When we resist change or try to assert a false sense of control over the external world, it always leads to struggle. We must learn to embrace change, work with energies and "allow" circumstances, opportunities, etc. to manifest according to divine providence.

The ego's need for a false sense of control can block the flow of positive energy that will actually bring you the ideal circumstances you are searching for. It is fear-based thinking and can undermine your progress in all the other areas if you don't recognize it.

The Law of Relativity

It is what it is. Nothing is good, bad, big, small, etc. until it has been experienced and compared to something else.

This Law also tells us that sometimes "s**t happens" ;) Energy is always manifesting—period.

This Law teaches that every soul will face some challenges—it's what you do with those challenges that define you and determine what you become. You can "fold" under the pressure or rise above and allow your trials to strengthen you. Learn to use your life's challenges as stepping-stones, rather than stumbling blocks.

One strategy that works when you feel a bit overwhelmed, is to know that regardless of what you are suffering at the moment, someone has it worse.

Keep things in perspective. That broken arm might hurt—but somewhere, someone else may have broken both arms and their leg! "This too shall pass." In times of sorrow or adversity, learn to glean the wisdom and the blessings.

The Law of Polarity

All things have an opposite.

Day and night, masculine and feminine, joy and sorrow. Without one the other would not exist. When working with Universal Laws we use polarity as a way to determine our focus.

Thoughts and ideas that are not working for your highest good can be removed by consciously directing your attention to their opposite. Feeling sad? Watch a funny movie ;). If you feel angry, rather than dwell on that emotion, focus on what you can do to manifest its opposite. In this way you find solutions that are inspired and empowering.

The Law of Rhythm

"To everything there is a season, a time for every purpose under heaven."

All energy vibrates and moves according to its own rhythm. These rhythms establish cycles and patterns. Think of the seasons, all of which form a full year. Each season has its own purpose and function, but is a vital part of the full circle.

Learn to harmonize with the higher vibrational energies that you seek to attract. Raise your vibration through the understanding and practice of the other universal laws, and harmonize with those higher energies. Meditation is a means that many use to connect their energy to their source and as a result they maintain "higher frequencies" and that sense of connection throughout the day.

The Law of Gender

All things have both masculine and feminine energies—yin and yang. All things require space, time and nurturing to grow.

This law tells us that when we plant a seed (masculine) it requires time to grow and manifest (feminine). This is the law that requires patience and persistence and tells us not to give up before the goal is reached.

More awesome "truths" from Christin Sanders on Universal Laws can BE found at her blog: http://universallawsexplained. blogspot.com

Chapter 5

The Universal Laws of Reciprocity

"We change the world not by what we say or do, but as a consequence of what we have become; thus, every spiritual aspirant serves the world."
~David Hawkins~

There are many laws that govern our existence on this planet, and in our Universe, and The Universal Laws of Reciprocity is one set of them. They are gifts from the One Who Is, created and put into place to protect us from ourselves, each other, and to protect us from the rest of creation. I was taught these laws of how energy works from Sun Bear through the teachings of my most blessed teacher, Saundra Pathweaver.

The Universal Laws of Reciprocity

- **Like *Attracts* Like**
"You are a living magnet. What you attract into your life is in harmony with your dominant thoughts."
~Brian Tracy~

- **What You Give Out, Comes Back To You**
"What we give attention to increases."
~Cindy Prosor~

- **As You Believe, So *Shall* It Be**

"An old belief is like an old shoe. We so value its comfort
that we fail to notice the hole in it."
~Robert Brault~

- **What You Ask For, You *Shall* Receive**

"Intentions: I AM responsible for what I choose. I choose
the feelings I experience. I set goals that I achieve. And
everything that seems to happen to me, I ask for and receive
as I have asked."
~Malikka Chopra~

- **The Collective Consciousness Lives in Us**

**"You are the Collective Consciousness . . . it
has gathered within your cells and been stored
there by all of the ancestors that "built" your
DNA profile. You are the WayShower of your
ancestors . . . through you they are given the
blessing of ridding their "cells" of this heavy and
dense energy . . . they are enLIGHTened . . . and
flow into the LIGHT."**
~Ascyna Talking Raven~

Chapter 6

First Law—Like Attracts Like

Like Attracts Like is Mine
By: Al Diaz

"Everyday tell a different person you love them, even if you do it silently."
~Illumine Ao~

Having, living, and functioning from a Heartfelt consciousness has made a huge difference in my Life. I Love the awareness, healing, and empowerment it has brought me, and continues to bring my Loved ones and me. It has made me more grateful for all that I have, and what I am blessed with, including my opportunities. Living in this energy has caused me to move forward in a more insightful and powerful manner, with greater Self-awareness.

My motivation for writing this chapter came from my Heart, with the intention of shifting the energy for as many people as possible, including my Self. I trust that my passion for guiding people to fulfill their Heart's desires, dreams or visions will help motivate them to contribute to shifting the collective consciousness that is now becoming obsolete.

If you were to tell me the story of your Life what would you say?

Does the story come from your Heart or your ego?

Several years ago, my story would have come from ego and described some very uncomfortable relationships, challenging finances, compromised health, and deflated Self-worth.

The Joy that has come into my Life since I decided I had "had enough," and that it was time to express gratitude for all of my experiences, has been impactful in the process of shifting my Life.

I have to admit that when I am in the middle of "chaos" there are times I would like to retreat to where I was prior to the chaos, to when things were calmer. But somehow I keep pushing forward, so that when I get through with what is going on, I will be in the positive flow with the Universe and living with a raised level of awareness and quality of Life.

Shifting

I have been through the opportunities that are cleverly disguised as challenges, difficulties, problems, obstacles, and hurdles, wondering why they keep happening to me and what do I do next. My Life started to change as I BEcame more aware, and the momentum of change accelerated as my awareness grew. So this is my point: we must DO something to BEcome more aware in order to change our Life for our best and highest good, otherwise it just remains the same.

Innate Ability and Power

Every thought, spoken word, feeling, emotion, action or non-action creates a ripple effect. Not only in our Life, but also in the lives of our Loved ones and our future generations, even with people we may not know. The entire world feels the ripple effects.

That is how powerful our energy is, and the effect we can have on our Self and others, based on our thoughts, spoken words, feelings, emotions, and actions or non-actions. Every day is important, and all choices that we make are important.

Each of us dictates what our next moment will BE, our tomorrow will BE, or what our next year will BE.

When we fulfill our innermost desires it goes beyond affecting just us . . . it affects all those around us. Our external reality shifts, along with our internal well BEing.

I ask you to give this gift of Life your best through your thoughts, actions, words, feelings and emotions, because we never know the endless possibilities of what may happen next.

If just by simply BEing who we are creates our reality and our world, it is also the same BEing that recreates! Each one of us has the ability to recreate our reality, and our world. All it takes is the desire to do so, and to lead our own Life. The bottom line is that who we are reflects back to us from others in some form or another. Life is a mirror of what is going on within us . . . so BE the change or shift that you would like to see in others and in your Self.

Remember every thought, emotion, feeling, and spoken word we have had prior to this moment has contributed to what is going on in our Life right Now. But the beauty of it all is that we have the same ability to re-create our Life right Now for our future moments, days, and years ahead.

I am also here to tell you that synchronicity exists in every single moment of our lives. It is happening all of the time. It does not start, stop, and then wait for you to have another intention, thought or feeling to start over again. The synchronicities that are always happening in our lives come from what is going on within us. Our external reality is a reflection of our own attitudes, feelings and thoughts that we have going on within us and the Universe provides the resources or synchronicities to have them all come to pass. This is happening all of the time and in every moment.

Look at synchronicity as the end result of what is transpiring within you. Another moment in time that you have brought forth to your external reality from within you. With every event that is happening in front of you in that moment, you can connect the dots of situations, circumstances, thoughts, feelings and intentions that brought that event to fruition.

So as far as synchronicity goes, it happens all the time, it is happening right Now as you read this, because you brought it forth from within. This awareness will present more conscious synchronicities of what you desire and require because you are living in the moment. We all have the power, or the ability from within, to consciously create the lives that we desire and require. The reason some people seem to do it more effortlessly is based on their level of understanding or awareness.

Influences

We all have been influenced in various ways through experiences, people and practices. We have, to some degree, allowed those influences to dictate our Life, affect who we are or what we can do, or even question our intelligence. But right Now we get to choose if we want to BE different, and follow another path, a path that allows us to experience our innermost desires, and fulfill our destiny of greatness!

When we finally let go of our outside influences, and live by our most innate values, we experience the Joy that we are. By BEing conscious of all the external "stuff" that we have accepted as valid and also BEing aware of our true gifts and values, we fulfill our true destiny. This allows us the opportunity to *recreate the story of our Life* instead of replaying the same one over and over again.

So it makes sense that you make a conscious effort to surround your Self with the people who represent what you desire in Life. As many have said before, there is power in numbers, and having your friends and family, who already have the same desires you have, adds to that energy so you may co-create and have a fulfilled Lifestyle.

Bring into your Life the best possible energy, the best possible individuals, so that you can have the best possible Life.

To BE on the path of success, your relationships must be with people who are already on their path of success. The same goes for any path you may BE on. If your path is spiritual, then surround your Self in relationships with people who are on their spiritual path.

Whatever path you are on, whatever you desire to BE, whatever end result is to BEcome, having more relationships that match the new you, and lesser that don't match, the quicker and more at peace you will BE on your path.

So who are your relationships?

What are your resources?

Are they supporting, assisting, and guiding you to BE all that you can?

In my life, I see over and over again, that those who I associate with or the people I surround my Self with, are who I am or I eventually BEcome. It seems like that happens in all areas of Life.

Support

If you desire and require to live a harmonious Life that entails having perfect Health, perfect relationships, and the perfect amount of prosperity, wealth, and abundance, then there is only one place to go. There is only one place to receive, accept, and experience the influence from—your Heart.

It is that simple.

Your Heart already kNows all of the answers.
Your Heart already kNows what you desire and require.
Your Heart already kNows what is perfect for you in health, relationships, and success.

All you have to do is listen.

Also, when you are on your conscious path, you start meeting new people, like-minded individuals who resonate with you. The enjoyment and support you get from these new relationships can be exhilarating because you feel that they "get you," they understand you, and what can be better than that?

So the great news about letting go of relationships that no longer serve your best and highest good, is that as you allow the new relationships into your life that do serve you, they help to enhance your overall well-BEing.

Remember

If you feel it's time to move forward, and break the recycling of the unwanted pattern over and over again, then get the guidance you deserve from the answers you have within. Optimally utilize your blessings and opportunities for your best and highest good with the guidance received.

To have a path of ease and grace is to kNow and trust who you are, and what you are, and this comes through the understanding of Self-awareness.

This is done by a continuing process of shedding the old and BEing reborn with the new. In doing so you will welcome, receive, accept, experience, and bring all that you desire or require into your Life.

Raise your level of Self-awareness so you may bring your special added value to this world. It is your natural-born gifts that the world is waiting for, so I ask that you take it to the next level from where you are now for the best and highest good of all.

Anything that your Heart desires is possible,
and most importantly, you deserve it!

Listen, you can let Life dictate to you what is going to happen, or you can take your Life, and dictate to it what you desire or require, and evolve for your own best and highest good.

Gratitude

If you don't appreciate and express gratitude for the blessings (good things) and/or opportunities that seem like obstacles, challenges, difficulties, hurdles, or problems, your forward progress will create more of the same, and seemingly more easily.

You must recognize your blessings and BE thankful for them in order to allow more than what you already have, and also recognize your opportunities and BE thankful for them to move forward.

BE (who we are)

The natural state of BEing for the whole Universe, which includes you and I, is to expand, move forward, progress, and have some degree of success. But understand that humanity, or each of us, gets to decide or define the forward movement, progress, or success.

To BE who you are is to BE the person you were meant to BE. In other words, there is Love, Peace, and Joy that exists within the essence of who you are. You bring about these attributes through your original innocence which is your true Self, without external influences, and utilize the gifts, strengths, and talents that you were born with-which are different than the skills you have learned since birth.

You are special . . . you are unique, and BEing your true Self creates a ripple effect for the collective consciousness of our world by showing others that they also can BE who they really are.

Love is the power or the innate ability that is available to us in every moment. We don't have to seek it outside of ourselves or from anyone else. The Love of the Creator is our Divine right and is already planted within us . . . a seed that desires to always blossom, grow and expand. All we have to do is allow it to BE. This is the essence and the Life force of the Universe.

The bottom line is that who we are reflects back to us from others in some form or another. Life is a mirror of what is going on within us . . . so be the change or shift that you would like to see in others.

Loving others and your Self unconditionally will guide others through reflection to Love themselves unconditionally . . . and that all comes from the Heart.

What can be better than that?

All we have to do is allow it to BE . . . the essence that is the Life force of the Universe.

It is our Divine right.

When we follow our Heart, where the seed of unconditional Love resides, and which the Creator of all creation put there, we emanate the powerful vibration that we already are. The resources, people, and situations all come into our space and time for our benefit. This creates the momentum that assists us to continue on our path to what we desire and require in our Life.

Guidance

Here is a process that works wonders . . . and I suggest you practice this empowering and healing exercise.

Go to a mirror and look into your eyes (not *at* your eyes) and tell your Self, "I Love you unconditionally" three times. I also strongly suggest you do this exercise every night right before you go to bed, and every morning as soon as you wake up. This will enhance, and bring more awareness to your authentic Self.

Pay attention as often as you can, because all of Life or the Universe is continuously nudging you with every experience that you have . . . speaking to you softly or firmly so that you will remember who you are. But it is up to you to live in awareness, and in the moment to remember or to grasp that guidance.

Here is a tip . . . as you go through an experience pause and ask your Self, "What is this guiding me to remember?" and listen to the response.

The more often you do that, the more likely you will BE all that you were meant to BE. It is that simple.

Here is an understanding that works wonders: when you desire or require something in your Life, and you recognize it in your reality, pause for a moment and request through your Heart, "This is to BE in my Life for my best and highest good." If you did not have the knowledge of the experience in your being, you would not be able to recognize it outside of yourself.

You must emanate a certain vibration or energy to bring positive people, resources, experiences, and overall well-BEing into your Life. That is how you bring even more joy into your Life, especially when you are in harmony with what you desire and require for your best and highest good.

In other words . . .

We do reap what we sow.

Instead of chasing or forcing the end result you have in mind, express from your Heart what you already kNow to be true, or as you see it in your external reality because it already exists within you. The more times you do this, the more you BEcome what you focus on, which in turn, allows you to take the required inspired action, and then the resources, people, and experiences come towards you.

You are special. You are unique, and BEing your true Self creates a ripple effect for the collective consciousness of our world by showing others that they also can BE who they really are.

LIVE your greatness . . . make a conscious effort to fulfill the desires of your Heart.

Living From the Heart

Here is a thought.

What would our world BE like if we all communicated from our Heart energy?

I'm not talking about emotions or feelings, or all of the experiences you have had where your ego tries to convince you that they come from your Heart. What I am talking about is your original innocence, which is still within you, and has never been lost, regardless of what your Life has been like. That original innocence is still there, somewhere buried within you, just waiting for you to allow it to come out and do what it is supposed to do, and that is to *guide* you.

Here are three powerful outcomes we can potentially experience if we were to communicate directly from our Hearts:

- We would get out of our own way, and our ego would no longer be communicating for us.

- There would be no such thing as yearning for power or control over anyone or anything.

- Fear would ultimately be eliminated.

Consider the endless healing and empowerment that would exist, and the eventual Love, Peace and Joy that would BE the end result for everyone and everything. We would be living our innermost desires, sowing the seeds that were planted within us by a greater power long before we ever came into this existence.

Perhaps this can even BE the key to create the Kingdom of Heaven here on earth.

End Result

As you empower your Self by raising your level of awareness, and understanding of your existence, all of your upcoming situations, resources, relationships, circumstances, opportunities, and blessings consciously come to pass, and you will see them develop into what you desire and require in your Life.

If you desire that the global community or humanity BE a certain way, it all has to start with you. It all has to come from within you. It is up to you to BE the example. It is up to you to BE the pebble splashing into the pond, and creating the ripple effect. It is up to you to live and function from your Heart. It is up to you to Love your Self unconditionally. It is up to you to share your unique and special gifts, strengths, and talents and bring value to this world. It is up to you to finally wake up. It is up to you to do all of this, and end up having ego as your willing servant. It is up to you to realize you have the ability and the power to make a difference. It is up to you to know your greatness. It is up to you to consciously and deliberately create, and live the Life of your dreams.

I ask you to bring forth your best. Share the gifts you were born with, and bring added value to our world. Because at some point, when enough of us do it, evolving will be something we will all look forward to.

"Live Life with no regrets."

This means no regrets from the past, no regrets in the present, and no regrets for the future. Do you understand what that can possibly mean? It can mean:

- Unconditional Love
- Total forgiveness
- Empowerment
- Compassion

- Harmony
- Freedom
- Healing
- Success
- Wealth
- Peace
- Joy . . .

So in this moment and every moment henceforth . . .

- Confirm who you are.
- Confirm your original innocence.
- Confirm your own pure Truth.
- Confirm that you bring amazing value to our world.
- Confirm that you are the essence of Life.

And then just BE . . .

- A Life of healing.
- A Life of empowerment.
- A Life of blessings.
-

I ask you to evolve and live your greatness. Make a conscious effort to fulfill the desires of your Heart. Most importantly, feel yourself BEcome the perfect energy that is already you, the essence that you were meant to BE. Confirming who you are is not about what you want or think you need. It's about who you really are deep inside, living the experiences that will bring Joy into your Life.

For our best and highest good all ways,
Ilumine Ao,
Al Diaz

Chapter 7

The Second Law—What You Give Out Comes Back To You

A Genie . . . My Very Own Genie
By: Rev. Ricki Reynolds

"A genie . . . my own genie . . . the power of creation within me."
~Rev. Ricki Reynolds~

". . . If we share with caring lightheartedness, and love, we will create abundance and joy for each other. And then this moment will have been worthwhile."
~Deepak Chopra~

**"Your beliefs become your thoughts.
Your thoughts become your words.
Your words become your actions.
Your actions become your habits.
Your habits become your values.
Your values become your destiny."**
~Mahatma Gandhi~

This is one of my favorite quotes. To me, this profound utterance moves us from the inception of creation within us, to the ultimate outer manifestation of what we have created. This beautiful pronouncement simplistically explains both the truth and the path.

What you give out comes back to you.

Religions and philosophies around the world carry this same message in a variety of profound phrases and memorable quotes. The "Do unto others" concept is written many different ways in several traditions. I invite you to explore these passages as you travel on this journey of self-discovery and love.

Just as you are led to be here now, you are also led to the words and concepts meant especially for your own personal awakening.

You will find not only amazement in the similarities of these expressed truths, and a gratitude to the wise ones who have left these treasures for your discovery, but also you will begin to feel a deep reverence toward your own being and existence. You will look at the world in a different way. You will acknowledge the truth stored in your own DNA of your importance and opportunity. A passion within you will materialize to continue to pursue these truths. Your Soul will stir, bloom, and you will forever be changed.

What you give out will change.
What comes back to you will be altered.

It is a large concept to think that what we send out to the Universe comes back to us. We may have never really been introduced to the concept at all. The only remotely familiar example most people have goes something like this: "I made him mad," "I need more money," "I think I am catching a cold." Or, on the more positive side, "I am happy," "I can do that," or "I have enough." What is so powerful about these you ask?

Each of these declarative statements is talking to the Universe. They are proclaiming your condition and position. Even the specific language used carries powerful intent.

Thoughts, emotions, outcomes, and the degree of belief in your own worth and abilities in the Universe, are all revealed in every statement you make. When you think about it in these terms, liberation or fright can be found. It can be scary to think that the things you are most afraid of could happen, and the things you desire the most may never come to be. *And yet the most frightening thought is that you may have something to do with it all.* The journey and the outcome may not be to blame on someone or something else after. You begin to realize that YOU may have more to do with it than you thought.

The Beatles song Nowhere Man goes, *"Doesn't have a point of view/ Knows not where he's going to/ Isn't he a bit like you and me?"* How many times have you found yourself having a conversation about someone you know that goes like this: "It is always the same old stuff with them . . . same old story . . . nothing ever changes . . . if they would just . . ." Those words may not be inaccurate about the person in question. But we just can't seem to make the leap to looking at ourselves and seeing the same pattern. Or, if we do recognize the similarity in ourselves we are lost as how to create a difference. Perhaps we know how to create the change, what needs to be done, but we shrink from fear of change, or can't find the courage within us to make the change, and follow our path.

Again, we don't seem to have a problem declaring powerful feelings with direct intense intent when we accuse someone else of being a certain way and behaving in a certain manor. We pronounce: *They Are!*

"They are so ungrateful!"
"They are stupid!"
"They are awful!"

Or, on the positive side:

"They are wonderful!"
"They are so smart!"

"They are amazing!"

Our thought is precise, and our emotion is powerful. We proclaim their qualities, their abilities, their outcomes with no doubt, no question. We believe it when we say it—when we say it with energy and emotion behind the words.

Most of us don't understand this power or the creation it brings into being. We don't understand the power when we deliver this same conviction upon our own life and ourselves. We don't realize we are putting it out there to materialize in our body, our environment, and our experience. We think these are random "ventings" that hold no impact, when in fact, we are actually in the process of creation.

The creation of happiness or misery, contentment or discontent, having or need, health or illness, is ours. Here we thought we were just living life, having gains and upsets happening to us. We thought we had to react to the bad and hope for the good. We thought we were held back or down by other people and their actions. Not the case.

Just as you observe, feel and commit with power and intent when you speak of "others," this same power is in motion when you refer to yourself in a positive or negative way:

"I AM not well."
"I AM angry."
"I AM poor."
"I AM alone."

What if we rephrased these, "I AM" statements and beliefs in our mind and our heart and project this instead:

"I AM well."
"I AM happy."
"I AM beautiful."
"I AM capable."

We are often absent minded; carelessly and irreverently using the same verbiage in our speech as the Creator used to define his own being.

What you give out comes back to you.

One evening, when I was a teenager, my father was talking with me about the wonders of life and living. He said, "I want you to read the book, The Secret Of The Ages, by Robert Collier," he said. "You are old enough to understand these things, and they are important for your life."

He gave me hints as to the contents of the material. It actually sounded interesting, and I said I would read it. Months past, and he would ask me from time to time if I had read the book. I would reply, "Not yet, but I will get to it."

About a year past, and one afternoon Dad walked up to me and once again said, "Have you read The Secret of the Ages yet?"

I didn't want to disappoint my father, but with a slight bit of embarrassment, I lowered my eyes, and quietly replied, "No, not yet."

In his hands, and out from behind his back came a new copy of the book. With a forgiving smile he whispered, "This is for you. It will change your life. GO READ!"

I barely began to read when a paragraph jumped out to my young consciousness. A paragraph that affirmed small stirrings of truth from the earliest of my childhood knowing. It read:

"This is the greatest discovery of modern times-that every man has within him a particle of Creative Force, endowed with infinite Intelligence, infinite Resource; that he can call upon this Power at will; that it is as much the servant of his mind as was ever Aladdin's fabled 'Genie-of-the-lamp' of old; that he has but to understand it and work in harmony with it to get from it anything he may need—health or happiness, riches or success."

I thought to myself, *A Genie . . . my own Genie!* . . . This was another of my first real introductions to the power of creation within me.

A few years later I met a man by the name of Obadiah Harris. He was and is, currently the President of the Philosophical Research Institute, located in Los Angeles, California. At the time I didn't really pay attention to the fact that he had a Ph.D in Education, and a position with Arizona State University. Each week, I would listen to the content and teachings he discussed during the taping of his philosophy show at the cable station where I worked. He was a fascinating and well-spoken presenter.

As months of listening to these tapes went by, I eagerly absorbed new and expansive information about the mysteries of life. I felt like both Eastern and Western philosophical traditions were delivered directly to me.

I would timidly approach Dr. Harris after the shows, much the way a child would request a bedtime story from a respected elder, and ask him to explain a concept one more time, or to repeat a specific religious tradition. This great man, (no matter his schedule, or the important heads of Universities that might be kept waiting by his delay), would calmly, gently, graciously, sit down with me, week after week, and converse with my young seeking soul until I was satisfied.

I had a few things back then that deeply troubled me, and even though I tried to get over them, or around them, I could not. It was Obadiah, who one day at a luncheon—a luncheon I treasured more than anyone would ever know—first brought to me and my soul, the life changing awareness of the power of forgiveness, and the power of forgiving ourselves. That day he brought me hope. That day he taught me of my Divinity within. My eyes fill with tears, and to this day, when I think of this inspiring man with a reserved calmness, the teachings, and the gifts he gave me. I recognized his greatness, and he reminded me of mine.

These were my beginnings.

And now I AM here. I AM with you. Let me help remind you of your Divinity.

We have the power of creation within us.

We have the formula of creation already created for us. We have the responsibility of choice. Let's begin by looking at our physical being.

Our bodies are made up of an average of 50 to 75 trillion cells. Cells are the smallest structural unit of our body. Our cells are able to react to stimuli, transform nutrients into energy, grow, and reproduce. *We create within ourselves first.* Science now tells us that when we think negative thoughts or feel negative emotions, chemicals are produced in our bodies that weaken our immune system. In an article by Jennifer Read Hawthorne, called, "Change Your Thoughts, Change Your World," she states, "Humans have between 12,000 and 60,000 thoughts per day, and up to 80% of them are negative."

Metabolic acids are produced in our body as a result of negative thoughts and emotions. These acids are removed from our bloodstream in our body's attempt to maintain the blood's pH balance. If the body is unable to eliminate these acids from our system, they overflow into our tissues and systems causing illness and disease. Headaches, indigestion, and more serious illnesses like fibromyalgia, heart attacks, and cancer, all have beginnings in our cells, and their reaction to our thought and emotions. In the book <u>Biology of Belief,</u> by Bruce Lipton, PhD, (p146) cites: ". . . Our cells are not able to grow and protect at the same time."

When we bombard ourselves with negative thoughts and feelings of stress, a portion of our cells move to a protection mode and are no longer able to provide energy. Dr. Lipton states, "You can survive while under stress, but chronic inhibition of growth mechanisms severely compromises your vitality." He goes on to say, "To fully thrive, we must not only eliminate the stressors but also actively seek joyful, loving, fulfilling lives that stimulate growth processes."

Our immune system can be strengthened or weakened by the power of our thoughts.

William James, an American psychologist, philosopher and physician of the late 1800's, stated, "The greatest discovery of my generation is that a human being can alter his life by altering his attitudes."

There was a time when people would not believe medicine could use light and sound to heal. Yet today ultrasound and laser light are routinely used in medicine.

Each one of us has the ability to create first on the most personal of level. *We create within ourselves.*

With the power of our own thought, emotion and action, what we give out, comes back to us, first within our own being.

Before we create our environment or outcomes, we create our internal environment and outcomes. We can make ourselves sick, or healthy.

Our voice is another powerful sound. It creates vibrations and energy. It carries intent. It can uplift or destroy. It speaks to the universe.

The Creators Word called existence into being.

Our voice is a gift the Creator gave to us, and we use it to create, to manifest into being. Isaiah 55.11 reads: "So shall my word be that goes out of my mouth; it shall not return to me empty, but it shall accomplish that which I purpose, and shall succeed in the thing for which I sent it."

The words we choose are significant and have significant consequence. We can condemn ourselves to defeat with words that bear negative intent and belief such as, "I can't," or "I won't." We can create and overcome with words of triumph and praise, such as, "I can," or "I will."

Thoughts and emotions are comprised of words and sounds and vibrations.

Science has shown our cells recoil from negativity, and thrive in the presence of positive reassurance. Thoughts, emotions and words of love, acceptance, and forgiveness, carry healing vibrations, intent and creation.

Choose words that focus on what CAN be done rather than those that speak of what CAN'T. Choose words that are life affirming for you and your world and those you love. Contemplate possibilities rather than impossibilities.

What we give out shall come back to us.

Just as your body is the first creation of manifestation, we create our environment and circumstance as well. We mistakenly believe we can only create ourselves, and our environment, if the canvas is clean. This is not true. We can recreate any landscape. We can softly add details or remove or change images to better serve us and blend with our Soul.

The palate belongs to us. The Creator has provided us the paint. We do not create everything, for we were born into creation. We do, however, have access to this creation. We Co-Create. Our physical senses experience it. Our mind discovers it. Our Soul feels it.

Eternity is created one moment at a time. We have the power and opportunity to create this moment. We master the goal we have set in the present, and in doing so we create eternity, one step at a time.

What we give out comes back to us.

You did not create the universe you live in. You may not create every situation or health condition you find yourself in. At times, these experiences come to us as part of a shared manifestation for the good of one you know or meet. You may face a health crisis as a result of an environmental cause you are susceptible to in your human condition. You may have made a commitment in another realm that is currently hidden from you, to learn a lesson for the betterment and advancement of yours and others' higher goods. In these instances and circumstances, it is equally important to use the formula for truth. While the path of self-created, co-creation may not be fully possible during these times, we can still master a chosen self-created, safe passage and advancement of our Soul, through the experience.

We can choose our thoughts, our feelings, our actions, and our release.

We can choose how we honor ourselves, those around us, our circumstance and our environment, as we travel through the experience. We can choose and co-create the intent of our path and our outcome. *The limitations of the current realm do not limit our intent.* In the words of Anne Frank, in Diary of a Young Girl, "I don't think of all the misery but of the beauty that still remains."

I know that once you begin to discover you can be a co-creator of your world, once you discover that you already ARE a co-creator of your world, the questions still remain: "What steps do I need to take to change my thoughts, to change my process, to change my outcomes? How do I get there from here?"

I remember this transition time in my own life. In fact, it began at a time I was feeling lost and down. I wondered how I wound up in this space because for so much of my life I had an absolute knowledge I was special and protected. I knew there were basic rules for humanity overall; however, I had always believed that life was quite personal as well. It didn't matter how many people there were in the world; I was special too, just as they were. What happened to me? How did I get so disconnected?

I remembered moments of "magic" in my life. I knew these manifestations had been real. I also knew I had not been able to figure out how to consistently duplicate the magic. At this point in my life I did not feel special, and had not experienced the uplifting sense of magic in quite a while. I felt loss. As I pondered, I was able to recognize pieces of a formula I thought had once been in place. Still I knew some answers were missing. What I did know was I did not want to remain in this space.

I thought about people I admired and the qualities they not only portrayed, but also embodied. These people were successful, accomplished, well rounded, and balanced. They were financially secure and productive. But beyond all else, they were positive in nature, positive in speech, positive in actions. These people not only did not let obstacles get them down or keep them from obtaining their goals, they didn't even let obstacles appear as obstacles! They simply looked upon them as another task to be worked through.

These magnificent people, these inspiring souls, these secret mentors of mine, all had smiles on their faces. They had an easy energy and magnetic personalities. They drew people to them with a calmness and peace you could feel in your own soul. They oozed with can-do attitude. Their eyes smiled, their tone of voice filled with uplifting encouragement. These people exuded an energy field of light I actually could feel. I wanted to feel that way more.

Some were famous, others were not. The Dalai Lama is one of these radiant spirits. Deepak Chopra is another. I thought about all they were able to create, and at times overcome, all with the best of attitude and expectation. I not only wanted to study and be around these people, I wanted to BE one of these people. They made their desires a reality. They *knew* it was not only possible, but it was *doable*! And they *loved* doing it!

The world, and their life in it, was a connected, flowing dance of creation. I had recognized a pattern among all these people! Well, it was time for my answers and the picture to be clear. So I prayed, I asked, and I was lead. The following several weeks were consumed with reading material I was lead to read.

It was my summer of rebirth, renewal and hope. I felt affirmation in the glimpses of truth I had already experienced through the years. I was right! Something had gone on! I knew "magic" had taken place in my life from time to time. I was awakened to the fact that I had created many wondrous events and moments in my life. I realized these moments had not been haphazard. *I knew that I already knew! Wow!* What liberation! What confirmation!

During this period of my life, I felt angels and guides closely interacting with me. They assisted me daily in my awareness and growth to the next plateau of my journey. During this period, I was acutely sensitive to the reality of these expansive realms.

As I reviewed events of my life, I knew I had at times "fallen into" delightful manifestations of my heart. Unaware at the time I had actually had a part in their creation. I could also identify other instants that seemed to have been a more deliberate blend of thoughts, feelings, action and release. As if I truly followed a real recipe card and baked a real cake, yet, after the cake was made, I lost the recipe.

And then, in a few gloriously illuminated moments of my life, I experienced the euphoria of being the purposeful, credible, accomplished, conductor of my own harmonic symphony! Its music and feeling, resounding through every pore of my being. The musicians of my heart, mind, soul, and body, playing, in perfect unison, a powerful, moving song of dance and joy.

The movement of energy and the richness of creation filled my inner self and my environment with perfect manifestation.

The experience continued to flow through me and from me to touch others. This happened in a gentle flowing rhythm of love, light, and oneness. These were moments where I knew everything was right in my universe, and I was a deliberate part of it. I had been created with loving intent, and I, in turn, had created with loving intent.

These were the most magnificent moments of my life and the most humbling all in one breath. How absolutely Divine. From that summer, my knowledge continued to expand, my intentions became more deliberate, and my journey continued.

What you give out comes back to you.

One universal formula of creation: thought, feeling, action, release. You use this formula already. The goal is to be awake, conscious, and purposeful when using it.

In order to make something happen, you *think* it first. You say, "What a great idea!" After you have this terrific thought—this great idea—you *feel* so excited and enthusiastic you can't seem to contain your emotions!

You affirm, "I want it! I AM going to do it!" Next, you wholeheartedly plunge right into *action* to make your dream come true! Awe-wonderful! Finally you release it. Let it go . . . allowing it to come into fullness. This is the ultimate expression of Faith.

At last, you stand back, smile a contented smile, and observe your creation. You have just practiced the *Universal Laws of Creation: Thought, Feeling, Action, Release.*

I bet there have been times in your life you have had a thought, but could not seem to generate any feelings about it or for it. Thoughts such as, "I should exercise," "I need to visit Aunt Rose," "I have to finish cleaning the garage." These thoughts just goes around in your head for a while, and eventually comes to rest on a shadowy shelf of your mind. You revisit it from time to time, with the same lack of enthusiasm as the first time around.

At other times, you have had a special dream. One you have thought about for a long time. You have an ideal plan to make it happen, too! You have thought about it, and planned for it, thought about it again, and again planned for it again. Each time you think about it, you change it up a bit—make it better. You are going to take that class, make that quilt, and go see the coast! But something always seems to get in the way of really getting to it. Still at other times, you are in a frantic pace of action. You work and work and work. You work yourself into a state of exhaustion, with no real sense of direction or intent. Much to your disappointment, not a lot gets accomplished.

Or how about the times you deliberately set your mind's eye to do something, you feel passionate and vehement, and set into motion the needed action to make it happen, but then you worry and stress over it? You won't let it unfold? You won't release it into being?

Well, we all have done all of the above, whether we know it, understand it, or believe it.

All aspects of the Universal Laws must be present and practiced to bring about consistent, deliberate, creation. *And creation is creation, whether working for light or dark.* We all have more opportunity and more responsibility with our privilege of existence than we usually comprehend.

Okay. So now let's say even knowing the processes to practice, at times you have difficulty moving from a point of negativity in yourself, to a point of positive intent. Rather than attempt to change your attitude and perception from anger to acceptance, or from fear to confidence, first bring yourself to a place of neutrality. Trying to force the opposite emotion immediately seems overwhelming and beyond possibility for most people. And with good reason. Remember: emotions *are stronger than logic*, and that is why, at times, even when you know the where you want to be, it can seem difficult to get there.

Your thoughts tell you, "Calm down!" but you may still feel angry. Your mind tells you everything will be okay, and you still worry. Your brain says you can do this, and your fear still keeps you from taking action. You may need to stay in this space for a while until you can recognize, and work through what is keeping you from moving on to the refined intent of your creation. Learn the benefits of breathing techniques that change your brain waves to ones of focus and calm. Science has shown that quiet contemplation and meditation create a neutral conditional in our bodies, which creates no metabolic acids for us to have to balance.

Remember, some creations take time and work. Others transcend time, and are instantaneous. Once we follow the principles of the Universal Laws and formula, we must remember to be in alignment with the timing of manifestation for the benefit of our highest good. You probably have heard this expressed as, "All in good time," "Timing is everything," and "wait for the right time." You obey the Law and wait for the presentation of creation. The Universe is moving and arranging itself to manifest in the "within and without." The creation exists in the Etheric, and is moving to the physical plane in alignment with the greatest good.

The Universe also has the ability to rearrange itself instantaneously to bring into form a deliberate call for manifestation. We may know this as "miracles" or "Divine Intervention." The Law is compressed and executed in increments of time that can be difficult for us to completely comprehend, yet we receive the benefit. *Manifestation can be changed right down to our DNA.* The universe need not recognize size or time, it simply replies to us in outcome.

A good friend of mine once told me there was rarely anything as powerful in the Universe as a mother's prayer of love and request on behalf of her child. A mother's deliberate, selfless, undiluted humble plea to the Creator, with pure loving intent, for the safety or healing of her child, was one of the most pure, powerful expressions in humanity. The love and release, the trusting of her child, her most valued creation, into the hands of God, was to witness the Universe rearranging itself in a heartbeat. A mother's thought, feeling, action and release. Deliberate, undiluted, thought, powerful feelings, prayerful action, and ultimate faith. The power of creation in one of the most perfect, loving, and selfless forms.

I personally have had this experience twice in my life, and both instances involved my children. The one I am sharing with you occurred years ago. My little sister had lived with us on a couple of occasions. At that particular time, she was living elsewhere and I had been notified she was in distress, and needed me to come and get her. We lived 2,000 miles apart. My husband and I made arrangements to leave within 48 hours to bring my sister back with us.

The night before we were to leave, I was driving home on a 90-mile stretch of an old, two-lane country highway. On one desolate stretch of road, a couple of homes sat back a distance from the highway. It was dusk, and an oncoming car had their bright lights shining in my eyes. My vision was compromised, and before I had a chance to slow down, I saw a shadow run across the road right in front of my hood. I swerved to the right in an effort to miss the unidentified object, and lost control on the gravel shoulder.

I over-corrected, traveling at 55mph as I attempted to get the car back on pavement. I did pull the right side of the car back up on the highway, but by that time my entire Mustang was traveling sideways down the road. I saw everything in slow motion, as I screamed out loud, "I AM NOT DYING NOW! I HAVE TO GO GET JENNIFER!

I could see it all playing like a movie in my head. Several hundred feet down the road, the car came to rest on the opposite side of the road, down an embankment, and facing the opposite direction I had been traveling. I emerged from the car shaken but unharmed.

A man, who had seen the accident from his home, came running down the highway and down the embankment to render assistance. "Are you okay?" he asked in a frantic, shaky voice. "Have you taken professional driving lessons? Because I saw the whole thing and you should have been flipping down the road. You were driving like a professional to control that car. I was amazed."

My tires had been rolled over to such an extreme as I skidded sideways down the highway and embankment, that weeds and tall grass were embedded in the beads of the tires. The car had to be winched out of the ditch. But at that moment, my thought, feeling, action, and selfless release was so profound, that the Universe had rearranged itself in an instant. The next morning we left to get my sister. I knew the Universe had rearranged Itself in the beat of my heart, and I never have forgotten that moment.

Charles Fillmore said, "Prayer is the most highly accelerated mind action known. It steps up the mental action until man's consciousness synchronizes with the Christ Mind."

The Creator, creation, us as a creation and our co-creation ability is a Divine gift. As my husband Terry says, "If you are here, God intended you to be here!" This is the way in which we are all created equal—not by our wealth, circumstance, culture, education, or intelligence—but by the knowledge we already carry within. The knowledge is in our DNA. *The equal access to, and use of, Universal Laws and formulas is how we are ALL equal.*

Remember, you are never a spectator; you are always a creator.

The choice is WHAT you create. *Inaction creates just the same as action.* It simply creates a different outcome. Poor choices create, too. They just create a poor outcome. Unfocused, fragmented, and negative use of the Universal Laws still creates. It simply creates a less than desired journey, and outcome.

The journey is different for each of us, but the equality is the same. Your personal histories, your hurts, your traumas, are uniquely yours. These events and aspects of life are what manifest as your creation. They are like looking through a pair of improper prescription glasses. They distort your view of the world. These ills are what you must work through to find *veritas*—truth.

Explore, Read, Contemplate. Be a participant in the discovery of your personality, traits, habits, abilities, qualities, and triggers, what caused them, and how to improve and change what you want to change.

It does not matter how you arrived at the place you stand now. It only matters how you proceed. Universal Laws remain the same. Unchanging. You stand equal, every moment, every day. Equal and unique.

In closing, the most important message I leave with you is: invest in yourself. You are Divine. Your Creator created *you* with all you need for the journey already inside you. Your Creator has given you the spark, the formula and the ability to blossom to your full potential.

You are a Divine work of art, and as such, are able to create Divine works of art. *You matter.* You have purpose, you are light and radiance, and what you create matters.

You are unique.
You are a needed, necessary, beautifying being in the Universal Garden of Eden.

Your own special color and fragrance reaches beyond yourself, to give joy and service to the expanse of creation that lies within you. Live up to yourself, honor yourself, love yourself, and with quiet humility and gratitude, *boldly create!*
Be a verb!

Create, know, find, determine, alter, change, feel, believe, inspire, encourage, smile, begin, finish, do, and let go! Do all this with loving intent. The Aquarium Gospel 17: 1-7 reads,

"If one is full of love he can do nothing else than worship God; for God is love. If one is full of love, he cannot kill; he cannot falsely testify; he cannot covet; can do naught but honor God and man. If one is full of love he does not need commands of any kind."

Thank God, your angels and guides. Ask for assistance and focus. Ask for all you require. Honor and implement the knowledge found in the Universal Laws. Be humble for the access, and loving with your intent. Be the I AM you are created to be. Wake in the morning with I AM. Close your day with I AM. Be grateful.

Give out with love and joy. Just as you think and feel calm vibrations when another reaches to you with peaceful intent, reach out with peaceful intent. Be deliberate, clear, and undiluted in your thought, feeling, action, and release. *Miracles happen.* The universal laws unfold. The universe and your DNA will realign with amazing speed.

My prayer for you is an awakening into self-discovery, a respect and understanding of Divine Laws and formulas, protection and guidance from your Creator and Love and Grace through your journey, with intent create your journey, because . . .

What you give out comes back to you.

Chapter 8

The Third Law—As You Believe, So Shall It Be

Growing Into Belief
By: Naveen Varshneya

"The word "belief" is a difficult thing for me. I don't believe. I must have a reason for a certain hypothesis. Either I know a thing, and then I know it—I don't need to believe it."
~Carl Jung~

In the beginning, there were two types of human beings: "The Survivor" and the "Mystic."

The Survivor accepted his existence, and went on to find ways and means to survive by discovering food.

The Mystic questioned his existence, and went into the forest to discover the meaning of life by asking, "Who Am I?" and "What is the purpose of my existence?"

The origin of "belief" lies in a journey from "I exist" to "I survive" to "I exist, therefore, I survive." Apparently, there was no reason for man to care for his own existence, and try to survive by discovering food and protecting himself against dangers of nature, unless he was *driven by a need to survive.*

A need to survive was driven by acceptance of life in the ways it was realized by the Survivor. The need to survive became the origin of belief, which in turn became the mother of all the beliefs as humanity evolved.

The time and space spent in organizing humanity to live in a society where people created family, community and boundaries of nations, rests on the belief that we must survive. During this time, the human race evolved from "I exist" to "I want to survive," and life continued based on this "belief" until the industrial revolution.

Also within this time frame, humans had gathered knowledge on "need for food" and "need for sex," and had a good idea about the fact that death is inevitable; however, arguably, they had no clue as to the why and how these needs existed, as well as on the purpose of life.

Our entire modern world, until quite recently, organized and lived its self around the belief of "survival," which in essence, is organized around food, sex and protection. The birth of family institution, monogamy, community and political systems are all built around the belief of "this is what it takes for us to survive."

These survival beliefs were then passed on from one generation to another generation in the form of family custom and community culture, together with new versions of the belief as they developed. Although around survival, belief remained, by and large, the same until the Industrial Revolution.

Before the Industrial Revolution, beliefs were almost constant, or evolved in a linear, non-revolutionary manner, and were easily passed on from one generation to another. It was only through the birth of science, evolution of mind, and fall of religion, that these beliefs came under attack by the human mind exploring new dimensions of their existence, by venturing out and taking risks.

No matter what humanity did, it was still working on the belief that, "I want to survive." Definition of what needs to be accomplished for our survival has always gone through change from one generation to another, and one age group to another as humans matured; however, in a very linear fashion until the time of the Industrial Revolution.

As an example, a carpenter's child was bound to be a carpenter with better skills. This was progression of society, and this is how, within safe boundaries, humanity evolved, step-by-step. The "purpose of life," and sense of contentment really began to develop at this time, carrying with it responsibilities, and the need to bow to the mysteries of the universe, by worshiping and praying.

These formulating beliefs needed to be preserved and passed on as tradition; hence, *culture was created* as a mechanism, or process, to pass on the belief as: *Faith in Family, Politics and Community Institution.*

In order to educate need for food for survival, rituals of eating—three meals a day for example—were created, rather than letting people eat whatever and whenever they chose.

Marriage was created to regulate sex. Sex was identified as need, and that is why, in most of the old civilizations, like India, marriage used to be fixed by the time a girl reaches puberty. Boys and girls were allowed to live together in families only for a few more years until they began to identify sex as a need. This created a culture of early marriage, gave certainty in society, making men and women accountable for their sexual needs; else, they would have gone around having sex and reproducing indiscriminately. This would have created chaos in a fast evolving world where humans were leaving the tribal concept of family, and moving into ownership of women and their progeny. This new control became a survival need for man in the per-contraceptive era.

Both of these basic needs were regulated by creating rituals around food and sex. Cooking was franchised, as it would have turned fatal for the life of the people to eat randomly as they chose. Sex became institutionalized; else, it would have created havoc, had we chosen to franchise it like we did the food.

Apart from potential conflict need for sex would have generated with need for food, there was another problem. Who would bring up the children, and whose children were they?

Who would hunt for how much food and for whose children? Who would have sex with whom and when? The need for institutionalization of sex came into being. Body and mind were then cultivated to adjust around the needs of society, rather than the needs of the individual.

In this time in which we live, we do not question the need for food three times a day or sex for that matter. By now, we have developed a natural instinct to react to anything, which we believe is survival for us without questioning the source of the belief attached to the need. It is a developed instinct, and we do not question it working in a natural manner when we defend ourselves against anything we sense is hostile to us.

Society, religion, culture, and rituals are all external beliefs imposed upon humanity by the need to survive in a predefined format. These external beliefs acted as boundaries for society to evolve in an organized manner so that the need for food, sex and protection for the individual was granted.

The job of insuring that external beliefs continue to serve humanity was placed in the hands of political and religious leaders, and when they failed in their efforts to protect the rights of survival of the people, revolutions erupted and democracy was born. With the rise of democracy, suddenly every internal and external belief began to come into the spotlight of individuals when they discovered that external beliefs were no longer imposed on them, but they had a choice in forming their own belief systems.

It now appears that everything was working out to make humanity survive and evolve. The belief that "humanity shall exist and shall survive" developed to a point of Universal Law. Along the way, as humans began to get better with survival, they began to be triggered by newly-formed emotions: love and attachment at the birth of their children, pleasure at orgasm, sorrow on death, and so many other emotions developing on a minute-to-minute basis as the collective consciousness grew.

The answers to the questions of what is right, wrong, good, bad, acceptable, etc., that are based on our beliefs were attempted to be uncovered by "Mystics," and they experienced various explanations through revelations received while in meditation.

These explanations were rather difficult to comprehend for most people of the time. They, the Mystics, had to find a method for people to individually experience the truth of creation. Gradually, they formed a "rule book," and gave it into the hands of the Survivors in the form of religion. Religion went on to become the springboard where every curiosity and mystery rested, whether answered or not.

Through religious rituals, humanity was promised the ability to seek their own truth while living in survival mode, and of course, there were always support teams of priest and saints to help them deal with it.

Emotion gave birth to curiosity in life and vice versa. The drive for evolution of humanity was to have a quest for deeper meaning of life. It was driven by emotions, and developing emotions were where the "birth of the human spirit" was created. If not for emotions, humanity would have lived a very mechanical life, and the mind would not have developed to where it is today.

Emotions gave birth to desire, and desires became the driving force for the brain to develop, allowing people to experiment and work on uncovering their evolving curiosity about the meaning of life. It went on to search for answers to these basic question and many more:

- Why do I exist?
- What is life?
- What is the purpose?
- What is light?
- Who am I?
- Why is death inevitable?
- How is a child created and born?

In creating culture, and thus belief, emotions, or rather the capacity to handle emotions, played a pivotal role. For instance, because in some cultures men felt that allowing women to freely go out and mix with men was a risky affair, they created a cultural and religious "belief" to restrict them. This action was driven by men finding out their capacity to earn a living was challenged, and they feared loosing control of what they built as "home" or "certainty" to other men. Morality came much later as a typical survival instinct, driven by emotional need to handle uncertainty.

Every time emotions created situations of uncertainty, or fear of loss in the heart, or it was felt to be too risky to allow some situation to develop in the family, a belief was formed in the mind, and it was developed into a control mechanism.

While the mind was in this state of uncertainty triggered by emotion and fear of lack, the Mystic mind was being born in a human being to seek better emotional support and to sustain humans in a state of flux or uncertainty. Unfortunately this new developing system was being crushed in favor of survival. Had it been allowed, society would have evolved much faster.

This newly developing 'Mystic' belief system was a blessing in disguise for humanity. Women, in many cultures, were removed from the need-to-survive status, and allowed to develop the role of nurturer and homemaker. It became very natural for women to become the Mystic by living in uncertainty when their men left for hunting or war, and they waited without any guarantees that their men would return. They had ample time to live with uncertainty, as they banded together, and they became very adept at handling their emotions. Thus, gradually, every home was giving birth to a Mystic.

Today our women are giving that acquired strength to men to handle more uncertainty, and allow them to venture into the unknown. It is rare *not* to find a woman behind the success of a man. It is just so natural that we cultivated women to bring connection to mystery, capacity to handle uncertainty, and to support man in his endeavor to break a belief to achieve greater heights.

The Mystic realized that if humanity has to survive, it needed to find a way to help the Survivor plugs into the mystery of life, and the Mystics knew they did not have a real consumer product with which they could explain to everyone the way to develop belief through the power of faith.

All of their knowing was experience based, and the experiences could not be quantified. Worse yet, they did not even have a form and shape of what they were talking about to show the Survivors—nothing tangible.

The Mystics began to work on designing a system through which they could initiate the Survivor through ritual and ceremony, and help them grasp understanding of the value of life on the planet. It was important to give the Survivor's reasons to not kill each other for food, and instead convince them it is permissible kill animals or raise vegetation for food.

Even if the mystic did not know the full meaning of their reasoning, they had the task of explaining the concept of God to the Survivors, and that if you "sin" against "God's Laws" he is watching you, and will punish you now and when you die. Thus was created the concept of a Heaven and a Hell, and all the blessings and punishments associated with them.

GOD was given birth as a primary belief to humanity on which rested Faith. Faith developed into an emotion-based function, and as such, became implanted into our DNA for the evolution of humanity. It is important to take into consideration that in this current time, the erosion of Faith is possibly partially responsible for mental disorder and disease.

The intent of religion was very clear. It came into being to make better sense out of the life of Survivor, but it was not meant for Survivor to turn mystic in search of God. Developing Faith in the Universe or its mysteries, allowed human beings to fall back to "I exist." It is through the rituals of religious practices, that we began to have our faith in life, and accept limitations imposed on our life as a reality. Also through this interface with mystery, through religion, we began to fathom and get insights into our desires to demystify life further, and help more conscious evolution of the planet rather than unconscious evolution.

The intent of forming a Belief is a compulsive effort to move away from mystery. Mystery is uncertainty, and we are brought up to work towards certainty.

As an example, a girl is born and grows to be physically beautiful, and people are attracted to her for her beauty, and want to take advantage of her. Her personal need is to feel safe, but all people see is her beauty, and she may tend to form a belief that being beautiful is not safe.

If a person who has money drinks alcohol to excess and he does not fulfill his obligations and responsibilities to his family and community, another belief is formed, that money is the root cause of all evil.

If a woman had sex, and a child was produced, and no man was ready to take responsibility of the child, and there was no one to help the mother feed the child in the pre-contraceptive era, monogamy and marriage were created as a belief of what is best for women and the community.

It was believed that it was not possible in India to pass on their wisdom from one generation to another when there were no writing techniques. The civilization in India, developed the caste system, with the belief that people would excel if like lived with like similar people. People were classified in four categories of caste. These castes are: warriors, traders, priests, and workers. It was not allowed for people to change their professions or to marry outside their caste.

The system was to develop an organized way to pass on the wisdom from one generation to another, and achieve excellence in what they acquired as their skills within their own area of life. This system is very similar to the union systems developed in other areas of the world, and can also be compared to the development of religious control by others.

When a child is born in India, he is raised in compliance with external beliefs such as nationality, religion, and community. He is also taught compliance to his family lineage, consisting of family traditions and their values. For example, the traditions of India teach children to greet elders by touching their feet. Not to argue and debate with them, and to obey their elders in all things.

In other religions children are perhaps raised to develop and respect their own identity first before respecting others. Children in India continue to go to bed late at night when their parents retire, while in the West, children are sent to bed by 8:00 PM so that parents can have their own free time, and the child gets proper sleep and has his own space. Children in India have a hard time, trusting themselves as they grow up. It is hard to go against the elders of the family, or to venture a thought that goes against the traditions of the family unit. They are encouraged *continue to believe in the system more than they believe in themselves.*

To break such a belief pattern requires a level of reverse engineering and re-programing sometimes for centuries. We created beliefs in order to organize ourselves so that we could all survive. Johann Wolfgang Won Goethe, in "The Sorrows of Young Werther states, "We are so constituted that we believe the most incredible things; and, once they are engraved upon the memory, woe to him who would endeavor to erase them!"

As we gained more confidence in ourselves through religious practices or by demystifying life more than ever, we began to loosen our strict morality, thus our beliefs began to be challenged. *Morality is a police to belief. An instrument to insure belief survives and certainty prevails.*

There was very little need for common man to change his belief and experiment with uncertainty, as life grew from one generation to another in a more linear fashion. It is only through the fall of religion, birth of science, invention of contraceptives, and the Industrial Revolution, that we began to question, at mass level, and go beyond just believing to knowing. As stated before in this writing, this great change in our thinking processes occurred due to the fall in faith and mystery as exploited by religious and political institutions caused us more suffering, and began to erode away our belief in survival and what we knew about our lives. We began to question life at a mass level, within the growing collective consciousness.

This process has further intensified in the last thirty years due to the Internet, and our ability to communicate on a worldwide level.

Society was evolved by institutions to make evolution for survival as certain as possible. We did not develop emotions to handle uncertainty, and since components of mysteries were very high, we either accepted mystery as the unknown, or gave tools to humanity to delve into mystery to find the answers.

The key concern areas today are: "How do we handle survival, growth and learning in a non-threatening manner, so that everyone has a chance to evolve without infringing on the right to survive and lives of other people?"

"At some point, the illusion breaks down, and the opening for the start of the spiritual quest commences. The quest turns from 'without' to 'within,' and the search for answers begins."
~David R. Hawkins~

"The Age of Spirituality," as we like to call it now, has its roots in time around the Industrial Revolution, when we once again began to break free from the external institutions that increasingly failed to deliver on their promises. With the spread of a democratic way of thinking that took us practically from the time of the Industrial Revolution until the end of the last century, and continues today, a process began to empower every citizen, and give him or her control of their own lives.

In most of Europe, there are very strong social security systems and managed medical systems. There is the freedom to love without the restrictions of religion or culture, and people are breaking away from the belief in marriage to discover their own truth about who they desire to live with, and rightly so.

The right to food, sex, and protection from infringement of their rights is not a question. But the battle for personal and societal freedom from the shackles of the keepers of the beliefs is just beginning to heat up. The first rounds of discontent have been fired around the world, and we are feeling the pull of another revolution, a revolution that will shatter our belief systems of separation and privilege as never before in the history of humanity.

So if the question is not about food, sex and protection, what is the question? Could it be, as similarly stated previously, "How do we, as an awakening species, encourage the exploration of growth and learning on an individual level, without infringing on the rights of the other members of our species?"

With control now in our hands, having infinite possibilities and choices, we are now all set for challenging every belief to discover much deeper questions of our life. We are taking away the power and restrictions of the mystics, and sharing with each other through amazing avenues of communication, knowledge and understanding of the mysteries of the Universe. We are creating new and expanding belief systems never lived before.

In today's time and space, as survival is no longer an issue for a growing segment of the global society, there is a certainty that if you make choices for survival, it is no longer a struggle. And with this assurance, we as a species are rapidly reaching out to liberate the huge portion of our global population from the chains of poverty, disease and fear. With increasing liberalization of society, sex has no premium or liability attached to it. With the fall of religion, our curiosity is unfulfilled, and a sense of contentment we drew earlier by placing our faith in mystery called God, is eroding.

The mystic is getting integrated into survival on a daily basis, as we grow to know that *Spiritual Awakening is an essential for our survival.* While working on survival, people are beginning to ask deeper questions about the meaning of life. Every question asked about a deeper meaning of life or discovery of the purpose of life, is a question about finding out the truth of our beliefs.

The beliefs we have inherited through our cultures, our religions, or though the journey of the soul across various births.

The beliefs we developed within the environment of our childhood in this birth, and are now reassessing before we pass them on to our children.

There is an old story that speaks of man's self-discovery. It speaks of creating Belief systems of eternal value for our evolution as a species. And to be ever aware and watchful of what we manifest as Universal Belief, and share with our children. This is my version of it:

A wise woman who was traveling in the mountains found a precious stone in a stream. The next day she met another traveler who was hungry, and the wise woman opened her bag to share her food. The hungry traveler saw the precious stone and asked the woman to give it to him. She did so without hesitation. The traveler left, rejoicing in his good fortune. He knew the stone was worth enough to give him security for a lifetime. But a few days later he came back to return the stone to the wise woman. "I've been thinking," he said, "I know how valuable the stone is, but I give it back in the hope that you can give me something even more precious. Give me what you have within you that enabled you to give me the stone."

~Author unknown~

Through the ages we have evolved until, in this time, we have morphed into the "Mystical Survivor," writing the new story of our beliefs . . . one at a time . . . together.

Chapter 9

The Fourth Law—What You Ask For, You Shall Receive

Ask. Believe. Expect. Receive.
By: Marisol Dennis

"The scientific use of thought consists in forming a clear and distinct mental image of what you want; in holding fast to the purpose to get what you want; and in realizing with grateful faith that you do get what you want."
~Wallace D. Wattles~

There is a story in the Bible that beautifully illustrates this law of the universe. It can be found in 1 Chronicles 4: 9-10. Off the top of your head you might not have any idea of what story that is, but you may be familiar with the book, The Prayer of Jabez: <u>Breaking through to the Blessed Life</u>, by Bruce Wilkinson and published in 2000.

The "Prayer of Jabez" has become a "guide to life" that has touched thousands of people. It is entirely based on this one scripture from the Book of Chronicles in the Bible. Funny thing is, I personally think that the Book of Chronicles is probably the most boring book in the Bible (shhh don't tell my Mom I said that). It is filled with name after name after name, tribe after tribe, after tribe, going through all this lineage. It gets very tedious. Suddenly there is a break and the litany of who was born to whom stops to introduce an obscure man who is never mentioned in the Bible again. His name is Jabez.

"Jabez was more honorable than his brothers. His mother had named him Jabez, saying, "I gave birth to him in pain." Jabez cried out to the God of Israel, saying, "Oh that you would bless me and enlarge my territory! Let your hand be with me, and keep me from harm so that I will be free from pain." And God granted his request." ~1 Chronicles 4: 9-10

What is so special about Jabez that everything would stop to recall his story? He obviously had the courage to ask God for this blessing. That's special. God *did* grant his request, and that's *really* special.

But how did he do it? If I had to venture a guess, I would say that he probably considered it a done deal as soon as he asked. I imagine he lived his life from that point forward knowing that what he asked was already given to him. He didn't worry about it; he didn't fret about it; he didn't question it; he just knew it to be a completed works and it was. He asked for his blessing, he believed he would be blessed, he expected this blessing and he received it.

No matter what your background, or what your religion or spiritual beliefs are, this is a Law of the universe:

What you ask for, you shall receive.
ASK. BELIEVE. EXPECT. RECEIVE.

It was 2000 when I was first diagnosed with cancer and I remember my beloved pastor showed up at my door with a book hot off the presses. It was the end of April, and this book had just hit the shelves. Father Nickas handed me Bruce Wilkinson's <u>Prayer of Jabez: Breaking through to the Blessed Life</u> and on the inside cover he wrote, *"PRAY, BELIEVE, EXPECT, RECEIVE."*

Father said all I had to do was ask for healing and it would be mine. He did not want me to believe my results. He wanted me to believe my thoughts. He did not want me to believe the doctors. He wanted me to believe my words. He did not want me to believe my diagnosis. He wanted me to believe the Cure. Together we claimed the victory over cancer that day and here I am, 12 years later, still standing.

> **"Ask and it will be given to you;**
> **seek and you will find; knock and the door**
> **will be opened to you."**
> **~ Matthew 7:7**

Funny thing about this particular Law of The Universe is, you really do have to be careful of what you ask for, because what you ask for, you will receive!

I was told I was going to die from an inoperable brain tumor and I almost took the chemo that was supposed to prolong my life, but after reading <u>The Prayer of Jabez</u> I asked for complete healing and if I can quote Paulo Coelho from The Alchemist: "the Universe was conspiring to help me achieve it."

To make a very long story short, I happened upon a Brazilian rock shop in my town called Middle Earth and my sister wanted to buy me a healing stone. As a result my life changed completely. Gina, the shop owner, introduced me to Norma, a holistic practitioner, and they firmly planted my feet on the path of holistic healing. I was helped greatly by these two powerful, yet humble women. Norma worked on me regularly and I had much more energy and was able to do more things. It was great for my kids to see me more active, but I was still throwing up blood and having seizures.

I continued to believe my prayer request for complete healing had been answered. I never asked for healing again but I always prayed in gratitude. Before long the universe began to conspire again and I connected with Shairy, a medicine man from Ecuador, right here in Montclair, New Jersey!

The next thing I know, (and I mean literally next thing I know, because it happened so quick), I was on a plane with my priest and one of my prayer warriors to stay with this shaman in his home in the middle of the earth. Everyone thought I was off my rocker but Father Nickas reassured me, "If you expect the miraculous sometimes you have to be willing to look ridiculous." It felt like I had not planned this trip. I feel like it really planned itself. I feel like it was the law of the Universe in effect.

What you ask for, you shall receive.

When I was invited by the healer to come with a caregiver, I didn't even have the money to get to Ecuador. I didn't know anyone who wasn't working who could come with me either, except for my newly-retired friend Adie, who was out of the country at the time. In any case, I believed Shairy was sent to my life for a reason and so I accepted his invitation. I remembered how Jabez asked for what he wanted and he got it, and so I prayed for the money I needed to go, and a companion who could come with me.

Although Father Nickas always had a busy schedule, I asked him to come with me and hoped he would be able to clear his schedule. When he opened his itinerary he had two whole weeks that were completely blank! That was quite unusual, and so we took it as a sign that we were meant to go. It worked out that Adie would be back in time to come with us, I was approved for a credit card, and I found very affordable round trip tickets for the three of us. Next thing you know, we were on that plane.

What you ask for, you shall receive.

The flight was difficult to say the least. I got sick, and even though we were used to it, and knew how to deal with it when that happened, the blood flipped the stewardess out and she caused a bit of a scene.

Then we had a run-in with armed law enforcement during our layover in Columbia, because Father and Adie switched seats so she could watch over me in case I got sick.

Once we cleared it up and they got back to their right seats, it blew over. But it was scary! They were at gunpoint! I remember praying for it all to work out, and the mantra I said in my head the entire time was just four words, *"Thank you Jesus,"* repeated over and over and over.

Strange as that might sound, it was all I could think to do. I was thanking God for this journey, praying in thanksgiving for the complete healing I was receiving in spite of the blood, in spite of the drama, in spite of the fear, I asked, I believed, I expected and I received.

What you ask for, you shall receive.

We arrived in Ecuador, only to find out that a state of emergency had been declared and the roads to the shaman's healing center were blocked. We had no way out; we were stuck in the city of Quito. The shaman shared a residence there with an art healer in Quito, so that was where we went for the night. So there we were, a priest, a prayer warrior, a pilgrim and a shaman. All the plans we made were out the window, and it seemed as if everyone but me was really worried about what to do next.

I admit I did not know why our journey took this detour, but the great part about asking with intent is that I didn't need to know. I simply needed to believe. As it turned out, the detour was actually a well-laid plan that led directly to the path of my healing. We just didn't know it at the time.

The next morning, Shairy decided to bring us south, since all the turmoil was in the north. We went to see his healer friend who was also a nutritionist. He thought she could teach me things I should know about diet and cancer while we were waiting for news about the roads opening again.

Before I continue with this story, I should mention that when I first was diagnosed and decided on alternative treatment, I had an uncle that I tried to avoid at all costs. He worked for a pharmaceutical company and I knew he would try to talk me into the chemo. Contrary to what I thought, however, when he finally reached me, he told me about the macrobiotic diet and a place in Massachusetts called the Kushi Institute, where I could learn all about it. I ordered their books and starter kit, but the diet was difficult and so far from my Latino-style of food preparation, that, in frustration, I put it on a shelf and left it there. I didn't realize then that the universe was trying to answer my request and I was blocking my blessings. Which leads me back to this nutritionist.

We arrived in the south of Quito with an incredible view of Cotopaxi, the second highest mountain in Ecuador. We walked down another dirt road that lead us to the beautiful home of Dr. Rosa Araque Romero.

As we walked through the front door, there was a wall with built-in bookshelves encased in glass. On those shelves were round disks of different colors, and triangle-shaped paper that reminded me of origami. It was in all different colors, but something else that stunned me. It was a Latino-style macrobiotic cookbook like the one I had shelved, and she was the author!

Can you imagine my surprise when I found out that she even went to Boston and studied under Misho Kushi himself? My Uncle would have been almost as happy as I was. In that instance I realized that the Macrobiotic Diet was part of my answer for healing, and even though I blocked the blessing the first time around, this state-of-emergency detour was actually the universe responding to my request again. Only this time I heard it loud and clear!

I had just about given up on macrobiotic cooking, even though I knew it was best, and here I was, in the middle of the earth, in the presence of a macrobiotic pro to learn from. Shairy and I had never even spoken about macrobiotics, and yet it was to that house—that beautiful woman and her wonderful world of macrobiotics—that he was guided to lead us. It's funny how things work out; we were all a bit disappointed about having to turn to Plan B, when all along it was God's Plan A!

> ### *"Everything that you will ask in prayer and believe, you will receive."*
> ### *~Matthew 21:22*

It was quite a healing journey for all four of us. It was filled with the unexpected and unexplained. At every turn there was more evidence that the universe truly does conspire to help us achieve what we ask for. I learned so much from that journey. We are designed with this super-powered healing system that we break by eating the wrong things and by absorbing all the toxins in our environment.

I learned how to restore that system back to good health. I also learned how disease can affect us when we have deep seated emotional issues that are so much easier to bury than to face. The problem is, I prayed for complete healing and since what we ask for we shall receive, I had to face those demons too. When I got back home the seizures had stopped, I was able to eat again. I was no longer throwing up blood.

To this day, I live with an inoperable brain tumor and since that first trip to Ecuador, I've been in and out of remission several times. To this day, I also continue to live joyfully with a heart full of love and gratitude for my complete healing. The universe is on it's own clock. Who am I to question it? I have experienced complete healing in many areas of my life and I am still a work in progress.

Someone reading this right now may wonder how I can say my request was granted, if even I have continued to battle cancer? To you I say I am no longer dying of cancer. I am living with it. I am very much alive and instead of preparing my children to live without their mother over a decade ago, I am bouncing grandchildren on my knee. My strongest thought was to be here for my children, to watch them grow up and be with them through the important milestones of their lives. Yes indeed, my request has been granted!

I have even managed to rub off on my children and teach them all of the lessons the universe has taught me throughout this journey. Take my daughter, Gabi, for instance. When she was 15 years old she wanted to play the guitar. She already saw herself as an artist and a budding musician. She asked for the gift of music with the full intention of receiving that gift. And it was with a heart full of faith, gratitude and confidence, that she picked up a guitar, got on YouTube and proceeded to teach herself how to play. She was graced with the gift of music, and in turn she blessed others with her talent.

In 2010, Gabi was sitting in front of the computer when she excitedly called me into the room. Just by the sound of her voice I was excited too. That was until I realized what all the excitement was about. On the computer screen was a flyer for a Battle of the Bands.

"Look Ma," she said jumping and twirling, "I'm going to audition for the Battle of the Bands."

I didn't want to hurt her feelings, so I tried to be as gentle as I could. But Gabi," I said. "I think you need a band to be in the battle."

"I know," she said confidently.

"The Battle of the Bands is in a week." I pointed out.

"That gives me a week to put together a band and be ready," she replied. There was something in her reply that made me pause. It was not just her words, but her intention behind her words. I recognized it from my own intentions and it was then that I realized that she was so right and I was so wrong. As a mother I was just trying to protect her from failing, but the way she said so matter of fact, that she was going to audition for that battle, reminded me of the Universal Law:

What you ask for, you shall receive.

I remembered that when I decided to battle cancer without chemo or radiation, lots of people thought I was off my rocker. What they didn't know was I had already asked the Universe for healing, and it was in that asking I knew it was already answered.

I saw this same confidence—this same determination—in my daughter and I was so proud.

"Alright sweetheart," I said, "you'd better get to work." From the smiles on our faces, we both knew that her request for a band had already been granted.

Within the week, *Candied Roses* was formed and they had a wonderful audition. They've been playing together ever since. In fact, they were recently one of the winners of an Underground Artist Competition and will be Headlining at The Blue Room Lounge in Secaucus, NJ.

Gabi had a dream of playing and composing music. She saw herself on stage jamming with a band in front of a live audience. When she asked the Universe to make those dreams become reality, she never doubted that they would. Gabi's story of how her band formed is simply more proof that when you ask with the full intent of receiving, you will!

It's like my friend Karen, who lived in a tiny apartment and she was always so depressed thinking about all the things she didn't have. I would tell her to change her thinking—to shift her focus. And one day, when I went by her place and saw that all her stuff was packed up in boxes. I was surprised because I did not know she had gotten a new place.

"You told me to change my thinking," she explained, "so I decided to think about the new place I am going to have."

She had not gotten a new place to live yet, but she was all packed up in preparation for the move that she was sure would happen. It was that one little shift in her mindset that opened up that Law of the Universe for her.

It was her belief and her taking action based on that belief, which made the phone ring one day shortly after my visit. Her friend had to move with her job, so she was living with her mother in a beautiful home on 36 acres of land in Central

Jersey. She called to ask Karen to move into the house so her mother would not be alone. Not only did Karen get a big, beautiful place to live, since she did not have to pay rent, she even had money to spare!

What you ask for, you shall receive.

Asking the Universe for your heart's desire may not be exactly what you think. In my case I used my voice and everything in me to shout to the universe my request for keeping this mother with her children, but did you know you are asking things from the universe everyday through your thoughts and actions?

The things that we are thinking, the things that we do, those are the things we are asking for whether we know it or not. It does not have to be an actual verbal or written request; it could be something as subtle as a fleeting thought.

When we ask to be free from debt, we are thinking about the *debt* and so chances are it will only get bigger due to our thoughts. My mentor calls this "stinking thinking" where we focus on what we lack instead of focusing on what we desire.

The good news is that this "stinking thinking" can be turned around very easily to a brand new, empowering request: "Abundance and prosperity will abound in my life." Focus on the good things in life, and that is what you will be blessed with. Your thoughts, your focus, and your belief, or lack of belief, will determine the outcome of your requests.

The next time you hear the phrase, "Be careful what you wish for; you just might get it." You may hear people laugh it off, like it's some sort of a joke, but you will know it's not. It's the Law of the Universe. It is always listening and ready to respond to your request. It does not discriminate between a good request or a bad request. It will answer you according to your own thoughts, so make them good! Focus only on the best outcome of your request. Visualize it regularly with true intention and it will manifest.

During one of the times I was out of remission I was being called to the San Francisco Bay Area to spend some time with my brothers and sisters from <u>Ancestral Voice, Center For Indigenous Lifeways</u>. Part of the healing process was a purification lodge. Prior to the lodge, I was asked by the chief to make a strand of 200 prayer ties. The challenge was that every single one of those prayers had to be for my own healing and myself.

Back then, my brain was so full of "stinking thinking" that praying for my own needs and myself was just too hard to do. It felt selfish to ask only for myself. There were so many people who needed healing like I did, who lost jobs, spouses, children. Somehow I didn't think I was just as important as they were, or that I deserved to be prayed for too. Funny thing is, each time I snuck a prayer intention that was not my own into my prayer tie strand, those prayer ties would end up all tangled up without fail, and the chief would make me start from scratch.

It doesn't take too many of those "do overs" to realize that not only was it okay to ask for my own healing, not only was it empowering to have a strand full of *untangled* prayer ties each holding an intention for my own healing, but it was absolutely imperative to focus on my own true intention so that my request may be granted.

Throughout this healing journey not only did I keep my focus on the positive outcome I desired, I looked for and listened to the signs I was being sent. We can't just put out a request, ignore the signs the Universe sends us and take no action. We would just be blocking our blessings if we did that. If I did that, I might be dead, much like this guy . . .

There was an old man sitting on his porch watching the rain fall. Pretty soon the water was coming over the porch and into the house. The old man was still sitting there when a rescue boat came and the people onboard said, "You can't stay here. You have to come with us."

The old man replied, "No, God will save me."

So the boat left. A little while later, the water was up to the second floor, and another rescue boat came, and again told the old man he had to come with them.

The old man again replied, "God will save me."

So the boat left him again.

An hour later, the water was up to the roof and a third rescue boat approached the old man, and tried to get him to come with them.

Again the old man refused to leave stating, "God will save me." So the boat left him again.

Soon after, the man drowned and went to heaven, and when he saw God he asked him, "Why didn't you save me?"

God replied, "I tried. I sent three boats after you!"

~Author unknown~

So when we put out our request, keep in mind that miracles happen everyday, that the universe is conspiring to help us achieve our heart's desire and that we should be looking for and following the signs that point us in the right direction and lead us to our fulfillment of that desire.

> **"Keep on asking, and you will be given
> what you ask for. Keep on looking, and you will
> find. Keep on knocking, and the door will be
> opened. For everyone who asks, receives.
> Everyone who seeks, finds. And the door
> is opened to everyone who knocks."**
> **~Matthew 7:7-8**

Chapter 10

The Fifth Law—Critical Mass Creates The Collective Consciousness

The Serendipitous Coincidences of Life
By: Dr. Ashish Paul

"To reach up for the NEW, you must let go of the old. What lies behind you is not nearly as important as what LIES IN FRONT OF You Everything you've been through was preparation for where you are right now."
~Joel Osteen~

The Universal Laws of Reciprocity. I must have learned about these Laws when I was growing up in India. All these years I must have known, on some level the literal meaning of:

AS YOU BELIEVE, SO SHALL IT BE.

The dictionary definition of belief is, "Confidence in the truth or existence of something not immediately susceptible to rigorous proof; *confidence*; *faith*; *trust*." I never really read this definition until now, and I never really thought of this word until recently. Whenever I used to think of the word belief, I would think of it as a religion or religious sects or spiritual sects. India is also called the land of many beliefs, so I always thought of this word in that context too, as a part of the belief system of India.

Pastor T. D. Jakes states, "When you live in your past, you are letting your history control your destiny," and realize that I, like so many of us, had been letting my personal and cultural history control my destiny, because of the belief systems taught me by my family, the society and the culture in India.

The first time the word belief really hit me, or entered my psyche, was at one of the networking meetings I attended last year. At these meetings there is a person speaking or presenting a topic related to business. This person, or keynote speaker, was David Key, an NLP (Neuro Linguistic Programing) coach and business coach. He started his talk with the word belief.

David told us a story to illustrate his point about his belief in Father Christmas as a young boy, and how as he grew slightly older, and saw various people dressed as Father Christmas, his belief shifted dramatically. I believe that was the point when I really *heard* this word. It entered my consciousness. I had not been ready for it until that point in time. Looking back at it now, I think it was a time when I was looking for answers in different places. Answers for my slow practice, and answers for the way my career was going. I was ready for explanations other than the ones I already knew, because nothing seemed to be working in terms of my career growth.

Allow me share a bit of myself with you. I am an Ayurvedic Doctor and a Medical Herbalist. I see patients and prescribe herbs, diet and lifestyle along with yoga and healing. I have been practicing for a few years in the United Kingdom. During a short period of about two years, I gave birth to twins, and stayed home to care for them.

I am passionate about what I do, and believe in herbal and natural medicine. However, it's not the main system of healthcare in the United Kingdom. Ayurveda and Western Herbal Medicine is part of CAM (Complementary and Alternative Medicine), and are not available on NHS (National Health Service). People who choose to use herbal medicine have to pay to come and see me. Thus, I must find ways to promote my practice as a private business. That presents its challenges mainly because Herbal Medicine is not in the mainstream healthcare system of the country, and therefore, is not covered by the government health provider policies. David Keys thoughts on BELIEF intrigued me and I attended his two-day NLP (Neuro Linguistic Programing) workshop, which was fascinating! I have always been interested in the mind, and the way it works. The mind has so much power. We hear all the time the saying, "It's all in the mind," and I have now discovered this to be true for me. I enjoyed learning about the workings and mysteries of the mind, because I like to be strong. I like to feel I am in control of my mind, and the situations that arise in my life. Hence, all the systems that harness the power of mind such as NLP, psychology or any other brain-training program intrigue me.

> **"We are who we pretend to be, so we must be careful who we pretend to be."**
> *~Kurt Vonnegut~*

Being a Holistic Practitioner, I know that mind-body-spirit works as a synergistic continuum: this constitutes a collective of, "Ideas, conversations, contemplations, decisions and actions that result in mass impact: for the individual, family, organization, community and the world."

From reading this definition of "synergistic continuum," it is understandable how our personal and professional lives are very intertwined with each other. We cannot be just a professional nor can we be just a person in the profession. Although I started looking at my belief system for my professional reasons, it made its way into my personal life too. I questioned everything. Not that I was not questioning before, but my pervious understand of the Universal Laws of Reciprocity in my life was generic and a broad view of my life and the events that occurred in it. Now I am more focused on the 'source of the event' as it flows through my life.

We are not just our bodies or our minds, but mind-body-spirit, and they work in relation to each other. As a species, we started out being whole and then differentiated ourselves into compartments, and then back to wholeness after realizing again that we are one and function more holistically together.

Professionally and even personally, I know when I have a hypoglycemic headache, for instance, that I cannot think straight or work. I feel physically incapacitated, although it's only supposed to be a headache. Because I have had incapacitating physical "illnesses" that impacted my mental sharpness, I am able to see the same effects with many patients; how their physical diseases or symptoms affect them mentally.

For example, a recent patient of mine came in feeling down and somewhat depressed, due to her psoriasis flare-ups. They are pretty bad at times, and affect her confidence level and bring her energy levels down. She finds it so stressful, that the psoriasis is having a negative impact on her IVF treatment. With my personnel example, and my observations about my patient, it is easy to see how we truly are living in a synergistic continuum with our professional and personal lives intertwined.

During my BSc (Hons) Herbal Medicine we had a Personal Development Module that ran through all three years of training, which was loosely based on psycho-analysis/psychology. We used to discuss, and critically evaluate, our behaviors, our actions and reactions, through various roleplaying games in the presence of a facilitator. The idea was to understand our psyche before trying to understand our patients'. The exercise also demonstrated how they affect each other in a clinical setting.

In those days, I didn't like critically evaluating my behaviors, as I used to be very touchy, somewhat secretive, and naive. I was new in the country, so there was a cultural gap working in my life too. But now I am glad I did go through those sessions of self-discovery, because they helped me to better understand myself, and how I interact with other people, and appreciate how they interact with me.

"The Universe is always sending us little messages, causing coincidences and serendipities, reminding us to stop, to look around, to Believe in Something else, Something more."
~Nancy Thayer~

RE-SCRIPTING THE COLLECTIVE CONSCIOUSNESS WITHIN YOU.

With a personal development module, I started to look at the dynamics in my family, my husband's family's habits, various interactions between people, and their behaviors towards each other. One of the fascinating books I read during those years of self-discovery was Games People Play by Eric Berne, a psychiatrist writing about human relationships.

I also found answers in, Codependent No More by Melanie Beattie. It is another self-help book written about codependency in human relationships. One of the issues these two books discussed, further propelled me to look into behavioral patterns that I now know are called "Collective Consciousness."

This issue involving the Collective Consciousness created the tense and complex dynamic between my husband and his father, with me getting stuck in the middle. This old pattern of belief pushed me into a set pattern of reactions to a similar scenario every time. My *reaction* was based on my set of beliefs fed to me from the collective consciousness that I "gathered" while growing up in India.

My programing was that parents were always right. We must respect our parents, no matter what they say or do.

Once I married, as a daughter-in-law, it was my *obligation* to agree with my in-laws decisions and needs. With this programing in place about how a daughter-in-law should treat her in-laws, I often found myself at odds with my husband. They felt I should follow the directions and "suggestions" they gave me, even if it went against what my husband thought I should do. This created a point of contention between us for years. My confusion as to who to honor first, made everyone's life uncomfortable.

Even now, all these years later, this old cultural programming of the Collective Consciousness still sneaks into my life, and impacts it; thank goodness, to a lesser degree.

Every time I would react to a situation between my in-laws and my husband, I felt caught in the middle. I used to ask myself if there was another way to look at this situation, because my responses to it was not serving any good purpose for me or anyone else. It took me years to separate myself from this conflict, and re-ACT in a different way.

"No matter who you are, no matter what you did, no matter where you've come from, you can always change, become a better version of yourself."
~Madonna~

I would say my personal development module, along with a couple of other factors, helped me to change the way I would respond, and eventually, helped me to step out of that "middle position."

Sid Savana, who developed "Personal Development Training 101," explains the basis of this module of training:

"Briefly, analysis driven personal development is the concept that we can truly improve ourselves through a few different strategies—analyzing the data from research studies, analyzing how other people have achieved their dreams—and introspection, analyzing ourselves and the way we are."

One of the factors that gave me strength to BECOME ME, was physically moving out of my in-law's house. Living together has its advantages in feeling more supported, but living on my own made me more independent in every way, and created within me a sense of freedom I had never known while living with my in-laws.

My Polish friend, Agnieszka, was wonderful in helping me to feel comfortable, and less guilty about moving out of my in-laws house. I met her while working as an Ayurvedic Consultant at a Health and Beauty Salon in London. She used to work there as a massage therapist and we became good friends. Agnieszka shared the lessons she had learned about life during this time, and I still use her advice in my conversations all these years later. She shared with me wonderful words of wisdom about marriage.

She told me that the day I moved out of my in-laws house, I would discover the real person inside my husband, because when living with parents, men are totally different. People of Indian ethnic origin will understand this much better.

The second idea she shared with me, that I absolutely love is, "We don't believe in *husbands* anymore, and we are *partners* in a marriage in this time."

Up until the time she shared this great truth with me, I never thought of marriage like this, and I have found her words to be true. Especially her idea of men and women being equal partners in a marriage. I had always believed in the sentiment of an egalitarian home, but this teaching of hers made a remarkable impression on my young mind.

Recently this was once again verified in an Indian documentary on domestic violence. It is especially important to educate the public about the horrible amount of domestic violence occurring all over the Earth, especially in countries with arranged marriages like India. With our programming to accept the traditions of our society and culture, women and girls are being terribly abused and do not feel they can "step out" of this way of life. The documentary brought out that we must look for life partners, and not the clichéd pre-programed patterns of relationships between "husband and wife." As partners we step out of the old paradigm—the old programing of our parents, society, and religious Collective Consciousness, and begin to develop a new one that is healthy and life sustaining.

"A wise teacher once ask me, 'Can we decide to change what is currently not working in our lives in only a nano-second?' ... You bet we did!"
~Laurie Bauman~

WHAT YOU ASK FOR, YOU SHALL RECEIVE.

I completely believe now that nothing is co-incidence, and everything happens for a reason. There are things that I learned years ago, and at the time, I wasn't really sure why I was learning them. But they have proven to be a part of my jigsaw puzzle, and make complete sense years after learning them.

Spiritual Healing is one of them. During my BSc Herbal Medicine training, I started to get attracted to Chakras, Visualization Therapies, and Healing and Wellness disciplines that were not part of the medical model. I began to look at healing as an arena for looking into the mind, or within self, or even to connect with a higher self. Many of my friends in my Personal Development class opened me up to looking at these methods of healing.

These friends used to be so vivid in describing their dreams, experiences, and psychological interpretations of their lives, that I often felt very ignorant, because I knew nothing about these "methods" of healing and wellness. Some of them would talk about visualizations, seeing colors, and "feeling things."

I was intrigued, to say the least, and I began to learn about these strange and exciting ideas. Upon the recommendation of a friend, I took a course in Spiritual Healing. It opened up a whole new fabulous internal world for me! Until then, I believed I couldn't see colors within, but through this course, I was shown techniques that opened the inner world of BEING to me. The College of Psychic Studies, where I took the Spiritual Healing Course, has a wonderful library, and I began to read and explore books written on the subjects of paranormal, mysticism, spirituality, and religion. Some of the books that made an impact in those days are <u>Science and the Paranormal: Altered States of Reality</u> written by Prof Arthur J Ellison, <u>The Field</u> written by Lynn McTaggart, <u>The Alchemist</u>, written by Paulo Coelho, and various Deepak Chopra books.

I had extensively read Richard Bach, and Khalil Gibran during my college days; I loved them then, and love them now! At that time in my life, I had read them as a leisurely reads, without any objective thought about growth and learning. It's only now that, as I see these books, their teachings are coming back to me, and I realize that everything is part of a bigger plan. We've just got to allow the working of this amazing set of Universal Laws to bring them to life within us!

"Often you are so attached to your limiting thoughts, you don't even see how you are enforcing them. Do you talk abundance and then clip coupons? Do you complain when you pay bills instead of being thankful for what you received, because of that bill? Start 'paying' attention' and don't level-up . . . Vibration-up."
~Sharon Hess~

WHAT YOU GIVE OUT COMES BACK TO YOU.

As an Ayurvedic Practitioner, and a Medical Herbalist in UK, I am self-employed or and run my practice as a business. As with every business, I must promote and market it. In my early days of practice, it was a daunting prospect for me to think that I was running a business. Possibly due to my *limiting belief* that I did not come from a business family, and so did not and could do not, know how to run a business. In those initial years, when I was gathering skills to run a business, I read a book by Stephen Covey called <u>Seven Habits of Highly Effective People</u>, which completely changed my perspective about business rules.

These seven habits are:

- Be Proactive.
- Begin With The End In Mind.
- Put First Things First.
- Think Win-Win.
- Seek first To Understand Then To Be Understood.
- Synergize.
- Sharpen The Saw

The most important habit I learned from this book was *Abundance Mentality*. Simply stated it teaches that *there is enough in the universe for everyone*. I had this belief from my upbringing, but I had never applied it to a business module. Reading about these seven habits, I thought I could apply them in my business, because they are an extension of how I behave in my life generally.

I have applied these principles to my life, as well, and I am pleased to say that I run my business the way I live my life. I put in love, respect, honesty and ingenuity, and I receive the same from other business people. I have become a firm believer of the Law of Reciprocity. I get what I give to others, but I am not giving with the intention of getting it back. Rather I am giving, because it feels good and I know it is the right thing to do.

My parents are strict vegetarians, especially my mum's family, who are lacto-ovo-vegetarians or Indian vegetarians; that means they don't eat meat, fish, eggs, or animal-rennet cheese. I remember once as a child, I went to get something from a shop in India, and I touched an egg at the shop while paying for my sweets. I washed my hand a few times after coming back home, because I was always told that non-vegetarian food was dirty.

You can see how narrow-minded I was in terms of diet and vegetarianism, or strict and conservative. I still avoid eating at a restaurant where it's menu is heavily meat-oriented; however, I have become a little more flexible when eating out, or if I am really hungry and need something urgent to eat. After marriage, my husband, and my way of living in UK constantly challenged this belief. Now I believe vegetarianism needs to be consistently followed in all areas of life, such as wearing leather-free shoes, driving a car with leather-free car seats, not having leather hand bags and so on.

My vegetarianism originated from karmic belief, and in a way, I wasn't as much concerned about the animals as I was about spiritual consequences. Now, it's a spiritual and ethical belief. It's as much about animal welfare, as it's about reducing karmic burden. So, I have seen a shift in my dietary belief and karma, which is all due to moving away from one set of Collective Consciousness thinking and belief, to another set of beliefs.

There is a huge difference in the way vegetarianism is perceived, and practiced in the west as compared to the East. Here in the UK, eggs and fish are acceptable as vegetarian foods, but not in India. This is still very deeply engrained in my belief system, because I have been contemplating for a long time to give sterile eggs to my twins as a means to get more protein in their system. But I haven't yet convinced myself to say yes.

I am raising my twins as vegetarians like me, and my husband has suggested using eggs once a week. I wouldn't like my kids to develop a taste for eggs, and possibly leading on to fish or meat when they grow up a bit more. I am providing an environment where they are not exposed to these foods, so hopefully they will not develop a liking for them. But, if they grow up to like non-vegetarian foods, then I won't stop them.

I am finding it to be a rather strong belief to live with and adjust according to where I am in this now of my growth and learning about this Law that reveals how the Collective Consciousness' lives within us. When I was growing up, I always found myself making my own decisions. I never really thought of it before, but now looking back at my life, I am realizing that I have always felt my decisions in my heart and acted accordingly. Sometimes I do wonder where and how I get that kind of wisdom to make my decisions. My best answer divine grace, since I have never made any major mistakes.

My family is a very small family. My dad was the only son, and so was my granddad and my great-granddad. This low male birthrate caused my dad's side of family to be small. When I was growing up, I didn't have any cousins living close by who were the same age as me. I never had anyone to consult with about what I was thinking or to share the kind of things kids share with each other. For this reason, I am grateful for my friends in school and college.

A lot of my beliefs about life must have come from my parents and grandparents, and I now know they were very idealistic. There weren't any realistic parameters or a person to calibrate my beliefs with, and I have learned that life is not just black-and-white as my family believes.

It has taken me all these years to challenge my cultural idealism and puritanical views on life and relationships. I have learned by trial and error, that life is not simplistic. I had to figure this out for myself and learned it my own way.

I now see my cousins growing up, and discussing with me their issues about life in general as well as their love life, religion, marriage or work. I see the importance of having someone slightly older, and definitely not parents, to consult or discuss issues that young minds often have. I am not against consulting parents. I know most of the parents of Indian background don't know how to be friends with their kids, or are oblivious to the issues that their kids might be going through.

I strive to keep an open and mature relationship from my side, but my mum is slightly conservative, and my dad, who was busy earning a living for the family, wasn't really around for much interaction. My open-mindedness always met with my mum's criticism, and I always reacted the way I had programed myself to behave, then ignored her, and still did what I wanted to do. So, I love it when some parents and their kids have a friendly, and mature relationship between themselves, and when they are open about their feelings with each other. I personally am very open-minded, and don't like the typical rules and regulations of society and support an open dialogue in any relationship.

That's how I am with my twins who are only four years old. I am their parent, but also their friend and guide. I do not want to transform into an old, boring typical parent. Since having my twins in 2008, and raising them, I am constantly inquiring, testing and re-evaluating beliefs regarding parenthood and childhood.

Understanding my beliefs is helping me to understand myself better, and to address any issues I might have, because I don't want to pass on these "conditionings" and behaviors to my kids. I want them to learn and experience things in their own way, and be less influenced by my husband and I on many issues. As I understand, many of our habits are combinations of nature and nurture together. To me, this means every habit and talent can be willingly shaped by us in small or even a big way.

With my twins, I am nurturing what I believe is kids' innate ability, to love, to be affectionate, and respectful to everyone. Also, I am guiding them to be "hugging people." I have come to share this immensely important life sustaining action with them, because of living in the UK, and watching Western culture. I have seen kids and grown-ups be so afraid or sensitive to touching each other. It's as if they think it will give them some terrible disease if they open up and hug.

Even parents with children don't hug them enough. People just don't seem to touch or hug each other, and have even sadly become sanitized to touch. It is a great sadness that the most important action we as human beings, should share with each other openly, has become fearful and taboo.

I love this incident, which happened last year as the twins and I were walking back from school on the way to the car. We met an elderly, and somewhat frail appearing gentleman, probably in his 70's. He was walking with difficulty through the forest path that we cross to-and-from school. I always encourage my kids to say hello to everyone, and possibly give a hug, so they gave a hug and a hello to this gentleman, and their openness seemed to please him.

The next day, we met the same elderly man walking along the same path, and my kids said hello again, and started chatting to him. He asked them, "Are you the same kids who hugged me yesterday?"

I replied to him that they were. As the elderly man was listening to my answer, and chatting with the twins, started crying. That's when I realized the ability of love to connect people. I realized that possibly this elderly man was very lonely, and hadn't been hugged for a while. I also felt proud of the upbringing I had given my kids! They are developing into two loving beings!

Isn't it sad that so many of us are so lonely and untouched? It doesn't take much to love each other, and show our affection. Why are we so scared to hug people?

"Friendship is the Universal Spiritual Attraction that unites Souls in the bond of Divine Love."
~Paramhansa Yogananda~

LIKE ATTRACTS LIKE.

I seem to give too much importance to love and emotions. For me the whole world moves because of love. I find it absolutely amazing and magical that in this big world full of people, that two people can find something in each other that no one else can.

When I was growing up, and hadn't loved anyone yet, even then I knew that it was special to love, and be loved by the same person. And after going through love and life, I am even surer that it's extraordinary to love, and be loved by the same person. I absolutely love those people who find mutual love in each other. This quest of love seems to live beyond this life.

My parents had a normal arranged marriage in India, and I didn't see any other kind of "love stories" in my family to become a fan of love, but it was there in my heart. I was not able to find any example of love, the way I knew in my heart it should be, in the relationships of the people from my upbringing. I almost worshiped love, and people who practice it, but did not get to see and feel it until later in my life.

I sometimes feel as if I had bad and sad experiences of love in my past life or lives, because I have always liked sad movies or sad stories. Maybe there is some Collective Consciousness coming from past lives that are making their impact in this life of mine in this now. I thought of exploring it with Past Life Regression therapy. It may be able to guide me in the direction of answers.

I had one session of Past Life Regression therapy, but I didn't have any specific question for that session, and so there were no specific answers. I was also aware that the Practitioner was my friend, and I didn't want to reveal much to her. Since then I have heard from other friends too, that generally it takes more than one session to get an answer. It is fascinating, how we can tap into this Universal Consciousness, and get information about anything. Just like "icloud" it's a "consciousness cloud" that has all the history of everything. Perhaps these sessions will help me to tap into my Consciousness Cloud, and will give me more guidance into my knowingness about love, and how far back it originated for me.

**"There are two primary forces in the Universe . . .
allowing and resisting.
The Law of Attraction is a fact of life"**
~Neale Donald Walsch~

I used to be very idealistic when I was younger, and had a belief that we only love once. I also believed, and still do, that love—real love—is unconditional. However, with age, time and experience, many of these convictions are shifting, realigning and shattering. Now I have seen love happening more than once. I have seen love beyond the normal confines of society, and raising hundreds of questions on morality, sexuality, love and human relationships. Now it's mixed up with sex and the divine as Osho describes in <u>Sex To Super-Consciousness</u>:

"There is a way to go beyond sex, you can transcend sex—you can use sex and erotic activity as a valuable tool for self-discovery and transformation. When sex becomes something sacred, not obscene, not pornographic, not condemned, not repressed, but immensely respected, because we are born out of it. It is our very life source."
~Osho~

I love this whole myth and mystery surrounding sex being a divine tool and possessing the power to transform us into human beings, and not just human doings. Whenever the topic of sex comes up in a discussion, the issue of morality creeps in. I read this wonderful article by Charlie Lutes on Morality and Spirituality, and am in the process of exploring it more. Here is the website for you to explore it too, if you choose: http://www.maharishiphotos.com/lecture78.html
What perfect timing it was to receive Tony Robbin's CD recently from a friend, with a wonderful exercise regarding

beliefs. On the CD, Tony asks us to first identify two limiting beliefs that hold us back.

I chose one about career and Ayurveda and one personal. I recognized my limiting beliefs to be:

- Ayurveda is not in the mainstream healthcare system of the United Kingdom.
- People don't like to pay for private medicine.

The next step in the exercise is to *feel* the impact of this belief in five years, ten years and twenty years.

Then you asked to choose a strong positive belief statement opposite to my limiting beliefs to replace them, and my statements are:

- Ayurveda is the best healthcare system in the world.
- People pay as much as needed when it comes to their health.

The next step in the exercise is once again to *feel* the impact of this new belief in five years, ten years and twenty years.

It was wonderful to *feel* the difference in myself with these negative and positive statements! I really felt a shift at my cellular level, and the tremendous power my beliefs had to change my brain waves, and to change my very DNA. I felt extremely happy satisfied and powerful.

I think we are all on a journey of transformation throughout our lives, with dormant and active phases.

A lot of churning has been going on in this active phase of mine, and it has been very active for the past year or so. One of the things that has helped me is my connection with Naveen Varshneya, of Life Transformation Research Foundation (LTRF), and its various wise members including Ascyna Talking Raven, whom I have come to know over the last few months. A variety of spiritual based topics are shared amongst us in this Facebook group that truly enriches all the members lives. I have to admit, a lot of my beliefs have been shattered, and lots of them are in the process of being redesigned. So far this is what I have concluded:

We are on a journey as soul throughout our life and beyond. The path leads us to destinations that are often mysterious and unknown to us.

Many times we do not know the purpose of the direction in which we are being lead, because we cannot see the destination, and we must trust in ourselves and the Universe. Have faith that everything is for our highest good.

The Universal Laws of Reciprocity, like everything else, need to be used as a means to assist us on this journey, with the willingness to challenge how they are working in our lives, and the courage to make modifications or changes when and where needed so that the Laws flow smoothly within us.

"In truth I'm not my body, my race, religion or other beliefs and neither is anyone else. The real self is infinite and much more powerful—a complete and whole entity that isn't broken or damaged in any way. The infinite me already contains all the resources I need to navigate through life, because I'm One with Universal Energy. In fact, I AM Universal Energy."
~Anita Moorjani~

Chapter 11

The Sixth Law—Critical Mass Creates

Tidbits of My "Truths"
From The Planet We Call HOME
By: Jeni Lynn Allen

"Our subconscious minds have no sense of humor, play no jokes, and cannot tell the difference between reality and an imagined thought or image. What we continually think about eventually will manifest in our lives."
~Sidney Madwed~

Do you ever feel that no one understands how you are feeling?
Do you ever think, *"I don't want to think about myself right now?"*
There is no one blaming you for thinking these thoughts. After all, look at the world around us. It seems everyone hates everything. It seems no one knows what you're going through, and it feels like you are all alone sometimes.
That's what it SEEMS like, but that's not necessarily how it is. Actually, everybody is thinking exactly what you are thinking, and I would like to explain how I see it.
Allow me to introduce myself. I am Jeni Lynn Allen and I am honored to share with you:

The TRUTH About MY Truth.

Although I may no longer be a teenager, I can still remember what it was like to be a teenager. What an emotional roller coaster ride it was.

Three years ago, I woke up one morning to a realization that changed my life permanently. This in turn helped me realize that my teenage daughter would most likely experience all those emotional roller coaster feelings I had. Something needed to change, or she was bound to experience the same unnecessary frustrations that I did. What I had realized was the TRUTH. The TRUTH leads us to discover who and what we really are, not what we think we are. And that's exactly why I am involved in this project. To give you—

TRUTH
My truth into
Oneness
Oneness, for some reason we feel in everything.

I am very connected to the world, and all life around me. I have been for as long as I can remember. When I was very young, I loved looking out the car window as a back-seat passenger. I would always be delighted to see the moon. She was usually there to light the way, unless it was cloudy or she was "taking a night off." I always loved how she seemed to follow the car wherever I was traveling.

I grew to appreciate the moon as I learned just exactly how much of a companion she really was in my life. The ocean tides show how related the moon is to our existence. A friend indeed! That observation led me, as a child, to *look at every single thing that my eyes feasted on, as something that has a profound connection to our existence.*

Another example of my observations had to do with the insects. I used to watch ants marching along. It made me laugh how they would touch their feelers together when passing each other in a single file line. I studied them, where they were going, how some were carrying things in one direction, while others were empty handed going the other direction. I would follow them to wherever they were going, and I would find their home. It was so cool to me how they knew to organize like that.

I found myself a back-seat passenger in the car again, going along the road in a single file line to the grocery store. I laughed and said to my mom, "We are just like the ants. We go about our day in a line to get what we need, and then we go back home. Do you think the ants have families too?"

That was my first lesson in the responsibility I had in being connected to everything. Even the thought that an ant could have a family made me never want to hurt anything living, not even an ant.

Universal Laws

Understanding that there are rules/laws that everyone and everything follows whether they know it or not.

I remember one summer day when I was younger, enjoying the sun that beamed through the branches of the pine tree that went up into the sky forever. I had a discovery about gravity. Yes, I discovered gravity before discovering Newton had discovered it. I lost my shoe! I looked down as it fell back to where I had been standing on the ground. Of course, I hung on a lot tighter than before. But thankfully, my shoe took one for the team to teach me that everything does the same thing. What goes up . . . goes down, and if you resist or challenge that thought, you will certainly learn painfully.

There is a flow to every thing that exists. It's really not hard to understand. Just be still and think about these things, and how they relate to one another.

First everything moves, vibrates and travels in patterns.

Second, each sound, thing, and even thought, has its own *vibrational frequency, unique to itself.*

It's the Universal Law. Can you feel the vibration right now—within you, and on the outside of you? It's happening all the time. It must continue vibrating because it is alive, and you are filled with this vibration, and can't change that feeling of life and movement within you.

There is a communication that happens, whether we are aware of it or not, and we have an influence on what is around us, and happening within us. It just happens like that.

The Power of Thoughts

The unconscious rules that free us, and give us exactly what we want . . . or what we thought we wanted.

Thinking is something that we all do all the time. What is a thought really? It's not something that you can hold in your hands, or see with your eyes; it's something that your mind is doing all the time, even while you are sleeping. *Have you ever thought about how amazing thinking is?* I find it fascinating really, to have a thought, an idea in that space between your ears. What's even more fascinating, is that you can get that thought out of your head, and into this life so that you can hold it with your hands, or see it with your eyes. Its really magical don't you think?

My Nana, so wise and full of advice, once said to me, "If you are going to be thinking, better think about good things, otherwise you will meet lots of bad things."

When you are a kid that makes no sense whatsoever. I mean, when did I ever think about bad things? Thinking back now, I thought of *all kinds* of bad things not even knowing it.

Like worrying. The more I worried about something, the more things would happen to make me worry.

I thought one day, *What if my best friend moved away?* I became sad about that thought, and I thought about it every time we would say good-bye from playing. One day, not to long after I started having these thoughts, she moved! Did my thinking it cause it? Or, *was that the future echoing back to me?*

I'm not sure, but what I did do was mentally torture myself all the way up to the point of her moving. Thinking those worrisome thoughts were powerful and they were taking my energy from me!

Did you know thoughts are measurable amounts of energy? Would you agree that energy is powerful? If thoughts are energy, would you agree that they are powerful too?

There are negative powers and there are positive powers. Both work equally well. However, both do not produce the same results. One is constructive the other is destructive.

Constructive thoughts create positive energy that in turn produces positive results. And destructive thoughts create a negative energy that produces negative results. So think good thoughts always, in order to create and call more positive things in your life!

Don Shapiro says in Life Is A Fork In The Road, "A positive person never allows the reality of the moment to stop them from seeing a better future and climbing as many mountains as it takes to get there."

Thoughts also have different affects on the various areas of our life, like our health, relationships with friends, or even grades in school.

Let's examine how thoughts affect our physical health. We now know that thoughts are energy, and they are powerful. Either positively or negatively. Along with that energy and power of thoughts are also chemicals. Yes, thoughts produce chemicals. Good chemicals with good thoughts and bad chemicals with bad thoughts. Things like worrying, release chemicals into our body that affect the health of our skin. We may break out in a rash or pimples. Or these toxic chemicals may lodge in the kidneys tissues, and we may experience back pain or neck stiffness.

And when we are happy or blissful, our skin seems to glow. We feel energetic, like we could run a race. Have you heard people say things like:

- "I need to lose weight then I will be prettier."
- "I don't like my hair it's too curly."
- "I will never be able to try out for cheer leading."
- "I am too shy."
- "My sister has better eyes than mine."
- "Why are my feet so big?"
- "I will never run fast enough to win a race!"
- "I was born with no legs, climbing a mountain is impossible for me!"
- "These glasses make me an ugly person!"

These thoughts come from something I call "Lack Mentality." Thinking you are not worthy of nice things, or sometimes anything at all. Keeping yourself in this mindset is detrimental to your health and wellness. YOU ARE WORTH EVERYTHING!

Relationship Material
Relationships, "it's complicated" . . . or is it?

Are good relationships actually difficult to find? Or have we thought all along they are hard to come by? What if you looked at meeting someone as an opportunity to gain value in your life? What if every single relationship you have is of value to all parties involved no matter how brief? What if you believed that every single person that crosses your life's path has a significant value whether you liked them or not?

Consider this: that teacher that bored you for an hour daily, for an ENTIRE year had huge value in your life. And so did every single student sharing that same boring experience with you.

Consider that the bully you wished had transferred out of your class taught you moral lessons about how not to treat others. And think about the possibility that you gave significant value to the lives of each and every student and teacher in that room. Yes YOU!

Through that relationship you gave something for those individuals to take forward into this existence. Did you make a positive contribution to those relationships?

It all boils down to *attention*. Human beings (that's YOU and ME) love attention . . . we thrive on it. We do things to get it. Actually, we are addicted to it. Why not give positive attention to every single person you meet. And see just what kind of attention they give back to you. Try this. next time you purchase something, look at the name tag of the sales clerk and say their name, look them in the eye and say, "Thank you for your service and assistance!" Observe how you made a brief, but important sparkle of energy vibrate through them from the smile on their mouth, to their whole face.

To find love and friendship, you must BE Love and vibrate at the frequency of JOY. To find respect, you must be respectful. All that it takes is a positive loving and respectful person to emerge from within you, and you will attract the same types of people into your life, which will make for meaningful relationships.

Family Ties
Family, we all have one (or two or three).

I could talk for days upon days about all the wacky individuals in my family, including myself. Oh the stories I could tell! The good times full of laughing until your sides hurt. Stories of mystery on summer nights with all the cousins playing tag or hide and seek. And I could tell you about all the fighting and arguing, and sadness and wishing I had a different family. I would have not one single story to tell you if I didn't have that family.

My sister and I used to fight like I wish we never did! In fact I'm embarrassed to say that we never really got along at all until about three years ago, when I woke up to the life changing realization I mentioned earlier. There were many years of good loving and bonding that we missed sharing together. None of that matters NOW. What matters is that I have NOW to bond and have fun and love her! I know she would agree that these last three years have been the best! Because that's all I allow for myself now . . . the best!

I have met people that live on the streets who say they don't have a family. I wonder each time if that is true. Really? They have not one family member anywhere at all? Is that why they are living on the street? Are they really all alone with no one? Not entirely. We are all family. We are all here on the planet called Home right?

Those people on the street end up saying to me that they do actually have a family. It's made up of friends that they meet up with every evening to huddle together. So, we ARE all family in some respect. RESPECT . . . there is that word again! We are never really alone when we love and respect ourselves, and we are never really alone anyway because we are all ONE.

Here is something else I love about family—looking back at ancestry. Now *that's* a good story! If you like stories, check out your very own family history that lives inside you! Find out about all the cool people that made a difference, or gave their life. Or what about super-smart people who invented something? There are also people who were adventurous in your family, who were part of the discovery of new lands. Yes, you also have the scoundrels, murderers, and really bad people too. *And they are alive in you!* Along with all the cool things you are already, there are, instilled within you, all those brave, terrible, mean, super-smart, adventurous, inventive abilities too. You are everything that your family is and more! And yet,

you are not them at all, you can do and be whom ever you want
as well! You are you! Unique. Oh man! That is so cool! No one
can be you!

Socializing . . . Blech!
All those cute boys . . .

Socializing is something I didn't even try until high school. Junior high for me was the worst in the socializing department. However, in high school I sure socialized! Are you kidding me? All those *cute* boys? I learned quickly that you had to socialize in order to meet. And I indeed wanted to meet those cute boys! I also learned quickly about all those things that you hear about. You know, like alcohol, smoking, and drugs. I learned about decision-making, and who was a good person to hang out with and who wasn't. At some point, somehow, I can't remember how, I got into socializing with that "not so great crowd."

Oh yeah . . . now I remember; it was one of those cute boys that I wanted to meet. Sure enough that relationship didn't last long!

Think about using socializing as a really cool way to *attract people like yourself to you,* by being yourself. Don't change the awesome person that you are just to fit in, just because that's what you think socializing is all about. Instead, be the life of the party, and watch all the people flock to be around you, be funny, but not obnoxious, and make people laugh and feel good, compliment others—you will be a social butterfly! (Guys, that's a good thing)!

BELIEFS
There are empowering beliefs and limiting beliefs.
Each has an influence on our lives.

Beliefs are the acceptance of something we think in our mind to be truth. It may even mean we *think* it is REAL. Beliefs give us confidence, some times, and other times. Beliefs can be very restricting, and not productive for us. Beliefs are ultimately an opinion that we have created about something we learned. Beliefs could be something we may have been taught that is outdated. Or maybe its something we believe, because we have listened to a story that has been told so many times we have come to think it is *our* TRUTH.

So, now we believe something that is half true, or even an out-and-out negative truth?

What if the other half if is not true?

If it is not true I believe from what I have learned it is a lie. How can it be that a belief could also be a lie? Simply put, there are two types of beliefs: those that empower you and allow you freedom to be the best you can be and there are limiting ones. These are called *limiting beliefs*, and they restrict you and keep you from exploring new ideas, and your full potential. What are some of the things you *really believe*?

I remember my first experience of finding out something I had whole-heartedly believed was, in fact, a complete and total lie! I was only seven years old. I had lost a few teeth in my lifetime already. I was proud to say that to date I had earned a whole dollar with my previous Tooth Fairy visits. And so it was time again to put my tooth under my pillow very carefully so she would be sure to find it.

This time, I wanted to tell her "Thank You" for carrying that heavy money all around to leave children for their teeth. So I took time and wrote a letter as neatly as I could:

"Dear Tooth Fairy,

Hi, I want you to know I took good care and brushed my teeth. I have no cavities so far.

Thank you for the quarter last time. I saved it. I am going to buy a jump rope soon with the money you carry over to me. Thank you!

Love,
Jeni Lynn"

I had to ask my mom how to spell some of those words and she helped me. Sure enough, that night the Tooth Fairy left a little more money. Maybe it was my letter, or maybe it was because it was a bigger tooth? Either way, now I had enough to buy my jump rope, and tell everyone the Tooth Fairy came in the night!

Weeks passed, and life was good. My mom asked if I would retrieve her purse from the bedroom as she was on the phone and needed a pen. The phones were attached to the wall back then. :) So I skipped down the hallway, and into her room, and I thought I would be nice and just get the pen from my mom's purse. Reaching inside, the first thing I saw startled me. It was my letter to the Tooth Fairy, unopened with my tooth in it! My thoughts started racing.

Oh my goodness, my mom caught *the Tooth Fairy? Wait? Money was left for me? Why does my mom have my letter? . . .* And then *wham!* Like a ton of bricks, it hit me. I had been lied to. I sat down and started crying.

And here is why I was devastated. In my house, according to my dad, *lying would not be tolerated.* It was punishable by the belt! In my mind lying was the worst thing you could do.

I must have not returned for a while because my mom came to look for me. She knew immediately what had transpired. She tried to comfort me, but I had time to think and I was *mad*! I wanted her to know how mean that was to tell me something that wasn't true . . . and I knew that it meant *a lot* of things I had been told were untrue, like the Easter Bunny whom I *adored*, and don't forget Santa! He was a pivotal role model in my life!

I distanced myself from my mom, and I had a hard time believing what she said, and even other adults too! Turned out

ALL adults had been lying to me. Silly for me to react that way? Maybe . . . but I was a believer! We all know our moms and dads didn't intend to lie to us . . . and it is harmless really, isn't it? Having Santa Claus to believe in?

Needless to say, I never lied to my daughter about Santa or the Tooth Fairy. She knew from the start they were for fun and that others believed them to be more real than they actually were, and that this was a very limiting belief system. Do you ever remember learning that something you believed in was really not true? If so, what did you learn ultimately?

The TRUTH
We create what we believe.

I bet you have felt like you have no control over what happens in your life.

Your parents chose your name.

They chose how to raise you with their values and traditions.

They told you what to eat and when to eat.

And, in some countries even marriage is arranged for you.

You might be required to go into a branch of military because that's what your dad and grandfather did. And if you don't, YOU are letting everyone down.

I bet you have had ideas of things you would like to do.

Maybe a career path in hair dressing that your parents are appalled to think about ALLOWING you to do?

Have you ever felt like that? Like you just wake up, and do what the world says to do? All of these things may be out of your control, *but how you react to them IS in your control.* This is being proactive in the decisions going on in your life. This is YOU taking responsibility for yourself. This is the world hearing you say, "Hey, what about me?"

If you are feeling heartbroken today, and wondering why, I'll fill you in, and share with you something of great importance. It was *YOU* and *YOUR choices* that have you feeling this way.

Can you look back and see that it was all of your own doing?

As soon as *we stop blaming* outside influences, outside circumstances, everything and everyone BUT ourselves, *we stop giving away personal responsibility for our actions, and what happens to us.*

We are 100% responsible for our lives!

Remember: you cannot control what is going on with your family or your friends for your life to be perfect.

The only thing you can control is YOURSELF, because

"You have only two choices in life—change your attitude or change your location . . ."
~Jon Sequoia~

Your actions and thoughts are what make your world go round.

"Fixing" other people actions will not help you, because you *can't fix* them.

What if you woke up tomorrow morning and said, *"Today I do what I want, and it is going to be good for me, good for others. In fact, it will be something good for everyone."*

What if I told you we have 99.9% control over our lives, where we go, what we see and achieve with our time, who we interact with and so on. That other 0.01% is death itself, but I will only give it 0.01%.

Today, you could decide to make a plan to do whatever makes YOU happy!

I believe that our vision becomes clear as we connect with and listen to our inner voice. Observing our lives with awareness helps us make powerful, heart-centered choices:

- Are you aware of what makes you happy?
- What if you could find out what your purpose for being was?

- What is it you have to offer the world?
- What is that gift that we all have?
- What is your special gift?
- If you could control your beliefs and your thoughts to find out what your bliss is, would you?
- What would you do to be happy?
- Would you do anything for YOURSELF to be happy?

One of our most powerful tools is our feelings. Our feelings are our personal reminder system. Feelings tell us what thoughts we are thinking, and what actions we should take next.

"YOU hurt MY feelings!" This statement is one that some people say and think often. So much so, that there is a "defense mechanism" inside you that is "pre-thinking" every way possible to protect those feelings, and emotions from hurting you.

This "defense mechanism" will sometimes put silly thoughts in your head to influence your decisions, such as lying, spreading rumors and avoiding people all together just to protect YOU from feeling sad. Which usually ends up making you sad anyway, because often "it"—that "defense mechanism"—is deciding for you, and *you are not deciding for yourself.* And **now you feel alone on top of feeling hurt**.

No one likes feeling sad, and yet sometimes, if we let this mechanism have control of us for a long time, it can override our true thoughts and keep us so sad we can't see happiness anywhere. *It's okay to feel sadness.*

It's okay to experience emotions, its normal to *feel* hurt sometimes. Do you know why? Because *that's what lets us know we are alive!*

Once you feel those feelings, be grateful that you have the opportunity of reacting from within yourself to what's going on in your life. When you are feeling sad, you have a choice. You could choose to honor that sadness.

You could even throw a parade of "wallow and woe is me" if you wished! Or if you chose, you could move on. You could explore what made you feel the sadness and embrace it. And you could choose to see the positive in the situation.

Did you know that every thing negative that happens to you also has a positive way to look at it?

Becoming a master of our feelings is one of the things we came here to learn.

Think of your feelings like a video game. Pretend that your happiness is the pretty princess you must save from the "Monsters of Feeling and Emotions. Imagine each level of the game you play is an emotion or feeling like Anger, Joy, Envy, Exhilaration, and so on. What if you could master your feelings like you master levels in the game, and gain a special power each time you master one?

We could even name this game. *Life On The Planet We Call Home*. Just imagine your life like a video game with each level of emotions waiting to be conquered. At the very end, when you add up all the special powers you receive from conquering each feeling and emotion, you reunite with the beautiful person inside of you.

What happens when we mix feelings with what we believe? Applying your "good feelings" to things you believe in, is like pointing a tractor beam at what you believe.

Remember in that movie Star Wars where the spaceship would shoot a magnetic beam, and pull another ship into its cargo bay? The more good feelings you project like Excitement and Gratitude towards your desired belief, the more quickly it comes to you. And if you put real DRIVE with it or what I like to call PASSION, it's like magic!

When I'm on a roll of prosperity and abundance, I LOVE to keep going. When I'm in a slump, I often need some motivation to get me moving again. I have heard the saying, "a body in motion stays in motion," and I feel this statement is a TRUTH.

When I'm just sitting around doing nothing, I don't feel thrilled with "whatever" happens to come my way, if anything. When I get up and get moving, I find I can go any place, and experience anything I choose to experience, rather than by happenstance.

Being patient is admirable, but being lazy is not. Being eager and persistent about taking action, while being patient about letting the results come, gives me a feeling of accomplishment.

So I have come to the conclusion that the way to live the life of MY dreams is to bring it about with focused action. And be patient while watching the results come in. I enjoy having the power of momentum on my side, and I do my best to keep it there. I will be in motion, stay in motion, and live life on my own very best terms.

When you have your feelings and emotions mastered, and you have your beliefs *focused* on things that are true, and that are in tune with your inner most desires, *anything* is possible. I am speaking from experience.

I like practicing using good passionate feelings focused intently towards what I believe in. I *love* everything all of the time, and that feeling of love is like a magic wand. If a desire is in alignment with what is true, and what is good for all involved, then it will rapidly transpire! It will just HAPPEN.

I love doing it so much that I have made a career around it! I have fine-tuned my tractor beam, and now, not only do I make *my reality perfectly*, I help people to in-vision their reality, and obtain it.

I find so much joy doing it, that the people I help usually feel overwhelmed with sudden goodness. And then what happens? I fill back up with JOY, BLISS and LOVE, like a rechargeable battery because I can FEEL their JOY, BLISS and LOVE and PASSION, and it just keeps going and going like the energizer bunny!

Manifestation—
 What all this new information boils down to is the
 Pursuit of Happiness.

"Life, liberty and the pursuit of happiness," where have we heard this before? What were our forefathers talking about? Happiness ultimately is what it takes to live a healthy life with internal freedom. We know chemicals are produced with our thoughts. And happy thoughts keep our bodies healthy.

Scientifically it has been proven that *happiness is the way to fill our body with healing.* Wouldn't you say that it is of utmost importance, for your health and well being to stay happy?

There is something cool about the Law of Attraction. It's called *Manifestation.* It's what happens as an *effect* of *asking,* and believing your good thoughts! And *not allowing "stinking thinking" to make decisions and choices for you.*

Think about what you love, require, desire, and crave, and *keep* it ALL GOOD, apply the actions that you are prompted to make towards those things you are thinking about, and you will indeed *receive* all of those gifts HAPPILY from The ALL THAT IS!

Why? Because that is the Law of the Universe . . . the Laws of Reciprocity. It is what the Golden Rule is really all about.

We are all just mirror reflections of each other and things start arranging themselves for us when we begin to reflect back the good that is shown to us. Things start appearing the way they should be, and the things that are false or are undeserving, or are definitely not part of our picture and choosing, just kind of disappear.

Think of something that makes you happy. Something like your puppy, or that crazy looping roller coaster ride, or your cousin that burps the loudest. Something that makes you giggle spontaneously. Are you smiling right now? Can you feel your heart right now? Kind of glowing? Okay . . . now take that feeling, and think about something you really want, but *think it like it is happening RIGHT NOW . . .* as if it is already a part of YOU and YOUR reality.

For instance:

- I got a pay raise!
- I got asked on a date from that sweet boy next door!
- It is so cool! My brother and I are getting along together!

Now, keep that glowing heart feeling focused on your desire and keep thinking *exactly* that frequency of energy . . . that glowing feeling called LOVE, and sooner or later you will actually living your dream through the *power of your intention and focus*.

It works! You have nothing to loose right? I mean, you think already, so why not start thinking with a positive intention and focus to creating the life of your dreams? We can have anything we want then, and we know how to get it.

This also means that we can change what we already have. Most anything you do can be undone, if you don't like how it feels!

Did you know that nothing is permanent except energy?

Now, if you think about this statement, it's really liberating! It's like painting your bedroom. Yes, time and effort goes into painting a room, and even money might be spent on it, but if you do not like the color, you can always repaint right over the color you decided was not what you thought you wanted.

That's how life is. Really! It's very forgiving. It allows you to do and feel what you desire. That means even changing the things in your life that don't feel good.

Maybe you have a relationship with someone that is uncomfortable. Did you know you can change those uncomfortable feelings? And there are two ways to do it: Change your location or *change your attitude*.

Take this story for instance.

I have a best friend I met in Kindergarten. We did *everything* together! At school we were in the same class every year, we played every recess together, we walked home every day from school, and played all day after school.

Things were *great!* Until one day, a new girl moved to the school. She was nice enough, I guess, but she was a *little different than my friend and me.* She didn't laugh at the same things we did; she didn't like to get dirty rolling down the hill like we did. In fact, she just kinda stood and watched what we were doing.

My best friend thought that was weird. So she started teasing this new girl. Now I didn't think that was nice way to behave. So, I stuck up for the new girl, and my best friend got so mad. For the first time in all the years I had known my friend, she was mad and we were in a fight!

Oh my gosh! I was crushed! I thought I knew my best friend better than that! I thought she was really nice! So the next day I was hanging out with the new girl, because my best friend refused to talk to me.

In fact, now *I* was being made fun of too! My (old) best friend told everyone in school private things that only she and I talked about. How could she do that to me? And to make matters worse, I *didn't think there was anything I could do to stop her . . .* I felt so powerless.

Weeks passed, and now it was only me and the new girl hanging out in the library together, avoiding the crowd of kids that made fun of us. I really didn't understand why this was happening; I didn't like it at all. In fact, it didn't feel good to me. Even though the new girl told me I was her best friend, I wanted all of us to be best friends.

After several weeks of this I gave in. I couldn't see the point in *me* allowing this anymore. I wanted answers. I walked up to my (old) best friend, and told her how I felt. I told her in front of everyone that how she was acting was mean and that someday she might not have any friends of her own. But mostly I remember saying that *she would always be my best friend no matter what she said to me or about me.*

She started to cry. All the kids around us became really quiet, and then she gave me a hug, and said she was sorry. She didn't want to loose my friendship to another person. That's why she had caused the fight. After that, we all three became really good friends. In fact even to this day, we keep in touch.

An important part of changing uncomfortable relationships is to be forgiving.

Forgiveness is an attribute that allows your being—the the real you inside—the freedom to love unconditionally, without you putting conditions on how you will allow yourself to be loved.

When we hold anger and resentment towards anyone for any reason, we are creating a limited belief about that other person, and then settling for that limitation. When we believe this limiting belief we are holding onto a lie.

Ultimately, this one lie will attract other negative feelings from all around us, and if we choose to focus on them, we won't even realize they are living with us—inside of us.

The worst possible thing that you can imagine having been done to you has no affect on the rest of your life.

Holding negative thoughts forever is not healthy. Holding onto resentment can hold you back from a successful life, and strip happiness from you all together. Nothing in this world is worth loosing happiness over.

So, forgive yourself first for holding that energy so tight it turned to carbon inside your cells. And then forgive yourself for giving away your happiness.

You see, it's all in how you react to what's growing in your life right now, how you think about it, and how you take action that really changes your life. Is there anything in your life right now that you wish felt better? How about writing down a list? State the "negative" feeling. Next, find a positive way to think about the situation that you allowed to create this feeling in your life. Next, think of and write down the ways you can change circumstances around you? And remember, circumstances are *not* permanent!

My Truth about it ALL.

Make life more enjoyable by choosing to see more of it as enjoyable. Instead of assuming that what you're doing is unpleasant because everyone else thinks so, see if you can find a way to enjoy it. Much of what makes life unpleasant is worrying that you're missing out on something more enjoyable. Let go of that worry, enjoy the moment you're in, and feel the genuine beauty of life that lives within you. The distinction between work and play is nothing more than a judgment call. Instead of making that judgment, make the choice to put meaning and fulfillment into whatever you're doing. It's easy to feel confined by your commitments and obligations. When you choose, it is just as easy and just as realistic, to feel enthusiastic and empowered by whatever it is you must do. Your situation is what it is. However, the way you feel about your situation is completely up to you. It feels much better to feel better, and it makes you vastly more effective at bringing real value to life. So choose more often to enjoy and happily experience life on your own joyful terms.

Achievement flows from the inside out. To experience an exceptional life on the outside, you must nurture exceptionally positive values on the inside. You cannot be angry, resentful, envious or cynical on the inside and expect to achieve anything of value. No matter where you might attempt to direct it, your negativity hurts you more than anyone else.

The great thing is, you can experience an outstanding life if you constantly and persistently envision an outstanding life. That positive vision will itself drive your actions to ensure its own fulfillment. There is great and unique beauty living within you. Connect with it, acknowledge it, express it and watch as your actions create corresponding beauty in the world around you. Achievement begins, continues and culminates, with the vision of achievement that lives inside you. Fulfillment flows naturally and unceasingly from the integrity of your inner self. Keep that inner vision strong, and keep that integrity intact. The whole of life surrounding you is eagerly awaiting the full expression of the beautiful vision that lives inside you.

Obstacles are not enough to stop us. What stops us is our assumption that we can't get past that obstacle.

Don't make excuses for why you can't get it done. Focus on all the reasons why you must make it happen. Listen closely, and hear that YOUR dreams are calling YOU. Feel their pull, feel their positive power, and do what it takes to make them real. And part of "what it takes" is doing it together your dreams are my dreams, and together we get it done!

Sharing wisdom, sharing resources, exchanging energy, creating currency, supporting, manifesting in co creation . . . this is how WE get through the obstacles. :)

Obstacles are not enough to stop us. What stops us is our assumption that we can't get past that obstacle. The problem is not that we have too much of this or too little of that. The problem is, we're waiting for perfect conditions that will never come. The achievement that really happens, happens in the real world. The things that get done, get done in less than ideal conditions. Don't make excuses for why you can't get it done. Focus on all the reasons why you must make it happen. There will always be challenges. And there will always be something YOU can do to get beyond each one . . . and prepare yourself to be good partner in your relationships.

"One of the principal reasons why so many fail to get what they want is because they do not definitely know what they want, or because they change their wants almost every day. Know what you want and continue to want it. You will get

it if you combine desire with faith. The power of desire when combined with faith becomes invincible."
~Christian D. Larson~
(The Secret Teachings)

The more I worried about something, the more stuff would happen to make me worry.

Manifesting LIFE.

Pretend there is an open empty space in front of you right now. You almost feel empty, and there is a blank clearing in front of you.

That clearing in front of you is your future.

Right now you have a choice in front of you that you could not see before.

Right now you have the knowledge of what to do with that empty clearing.

That blank canvas is your life!

Right now you have the opportunity to claim personal responsibility for your life and how it feels. It is our deepest wish for you to take this new knowledge and power that you have learned and pursue your happiness. Right now is the time to commit to yourself the good life that you knew had to be there.

Make a wish for yourself this moment. Wish for your happiness . . . take the action to move forward and receive it.

Today is the day to look in the mirror and say, "I LOVE YOU!"

I want to explain to you how I felt when I realized this TRUTH about myself. This is the only way that I can explain it.

It was as if the day I was born into this body, it was given to me as a vessel of sorts. And as my little spirit sat in the driver's seat of this vessel I could hardly see over the steering device so I was given an automatic copilot just in case.

This vessel I'm in can soar high and do many tricks. I was learning how to fly this machine when I flew into a pocket of turbulence. In doing so, I hit my head and became unconscious to everything in my life that was happening.

My automatic co-pilot was there to save the day, and it took over steering my vessel for me as I lay oblivious to my travels. It didn't wake me up . . . it just flew in circles around and around scraping the mountaintops and causing wounds in my vessel from time to time.

Until about thirty-three had gone by, and my automatic co pilot flew into some turbulence and I woke up, feeling groggy. I was amazed at how the landscape looked from where I was . . . and I was surprised at all the scratches and wounds on my vessel. I kindly thanked my automatic copilot for taking care of this vessel the best it knew how, but said I would rather be the one to take over the journey from here on out. I checked out the forecast and saw where all the turbulence was. I made an itinerary of where I wanted to go with my life . . . and now I am flying there.

No one else, not the co-pilot, not even the cabin crew can tell me my destination. Only I am steering my ship. That's how it felt in an instant. I started laughing! And that is the TRUTH!

Here we are today, and right now in this very moment, we have arrived at the TRUTH. It does not matter when you are reading this; right now, you are in *this moment*. Life is happening right now, in this very moment. It is being created at a rate faster than you or I could possibly comprehend. And here is the most mind-boggling part about it: right now, in this very moment, *life as you know it is ending at a rate of speed equal to that of creation.*

So right now, *nothing really exists*.

What does that mean exactly? If nothing really exists right now then where is everything?

Everything that exists right now is really in the past. And where was it? It was in the future.

But in the future nothing really exists right? *Only the possibility of something existing exists.* So what about right now?

What if the worst thing that has happened in your life was not affecting your life in any way right now. You are very much alive! Anything that has happened to you is in the past, is _not_ who or what you _are_ right now.

Who or what you are right now is waiting to be created. You do not exist in this moment. This is really, really heavy-duty thinking, but I know you can handle this thought.

So what this means is, whatever you thought was your life is not . . . it is merely a part of the past.

Look into your future. What's there? Who is there? Where are you? Why are you?

You are beautiful creation waiting to happen.

You are beautiful powerful energy thought ready for LIFE.

You are the reason for a manifested life of unconditional love.

The choice should be easy, natural and flow effortlessly.

LIFE IS JUST THIS BEAUTIFUL.

Start manifesting the life you want right now!

We are you.

Everything, every single living thing shares ONE LIFE with you. It is of the utmost importance for you to feel that connection. And to *choose* to embrace all of the love that comes from Everything-That-Is

It is a choice to Be.

It is your choice to live, love and learn.
It is your choice to breathe back the gift of love to Everything-That-Is.

When you make a choice to *feel*, remember first to feel for the Truth—your truth—before you judge, before you discriminate, before you hate . . . remember it is *your choice*.

We must appreciate the miracle that we are here *NOW.* We must forgive all matters of the past. We must always look forward, keeping a vision of the good, loving and gracious life that we are blessed to experience.

Take this moment now and choose. We, as one, choose to achieve a life that flows effortless in truth. Let there be no doubt in our minds that we are unstoppable.

You are creation in this moment so pure and so full of truth.

Start now. Not tomorrow or early next week or when you have the time. Now is when your time IS. Use it now.

Sure, it's important to plan and to prepare. What's essential, though, is to put your *intentions into action.*

Even if you're not fully prepared, there's something you can do right now.

Even if you're unable to get it all done, you can get moving in a productive direction.

Action accomplishes more than just the immediate results it creates.

Taking action seals your commitment and puts you in a state of solid, indisputable effectiveness.

Action lets you see and know, without the slightest doubt, how capable you can be. Though it's great to tell yourself you can do it, action goes several steps beyond that and shows you that you can do it.

Your dreams and goals and best intentions begin to be truly yours only when you act on them. So stop just thinking about it or wishing for it, and step forward right now with real, solid action.

There is nothing more that you, or I, or anyone one else, in this very moment, has except for OUR OWN TRUTH, created from our own perspective.

Live it . . . be it . . . share it . . . teach it . . .
breathe it, and allow . . .
The Truth—Your Truth—Now.

Chapter 12

In Light and Laughter—The Beginning of Creation As We Know It

"Every achiever I have ever met says, 'My life turned around when I began to believe in me.'"
~Robert Schuller~

Somewhere in the early beginning of conscious thought, we became aware that we were separate and apart from the Whole of Creation. It was an exciting and thrilling thing to suddenly manifest and create space, time, feelings and thought. We created separateness. Why? Maybe we had evolved to a space of being within the great I AM and BEcame.

Imagine with me . . . .

. . . The beginning of your creation . . .

I . . . I am . . . I am What? Where am I? So bri-bright! What am I?

I am feeling. What is feeling? *(Confusion begins to be. Separateness is).* So much coming together of matter. I am feeling a "body." Body!

Think. What is this thinking thing? In all of time . . . wait . . . what is this time thing? What is this heaviness I feel surrounding me? Is it good and warm.

Good? Warm? Oh, there is, there is . . . ? There is a 'solid' feeling surrounding me. Me? Oh! There is an awaking of more, and *You. You?* We? What is this? Who am I? What is I? I AM—? More thoughts!

Facing *You*. Face? Seeing? Feeling? I Think! Wonderful! Feeling, thinking. Thinking to be Me! I am separate from You! Warmth on my face. What is this I feel at my back? Back? What is back? I will me to 'turn' and see what is behind me. *(Fear is created and manifested).*

Me is small. What happened to I? Facing the darkness? Me is alone, where did *You* go? It is . . . 'fearful' to be in the Dark 'alone'! So much absence of light—darkness. It feels like it is growing larger and deeper. Where did the Light go?!

I am surrounded by the Dark! Afraid. Wait. What is Dark? What is fear? Did me do this? Where is I, and where are *You?* Alone! So alone! No Light—no warm—no *you*. How could you leave me all alone?! We have always been One, how did we become? How did we become apart from each other? Think! I saw *You* before I became me, and *You* became *you*. We were One in the Light.

Are *You* still there, somewhere? Somewhere behind me? Fear surrounds me. Think. Am I alone, or has this 'thinking' thing that has been created by me, placed a dark space between Us? If I turn around, will **You** be there? Will the Light be there in front of me? Will me become I again? Can I be me and I at the same time? There is that 'time' thing again. Where did it come from? If I have a back, is there a front? If I stand in the Dark, is there a Light now behind me? What if I lost it, the Light? Can I loose the Light, and have only Dark? Are *You* still 'there'?

This feeling of loss, of separateness, is so thick in the darkness around me! That is fear! This thing I have created has left 'me' in its stead. I must turn around! I must 'face' again behind me. What if I turn around and find only more darkness? Fear continues to surround me! Think! Me must be I again. I AM . . . that being of Light. If I created the me of darkness, I AM that, and the Light also! Turn! Turn around. Think . . . *the Light is there*. Think . . . *the Light never left me; I left it behind me.*

Turn?! Fear! Fear clutches at me as thick as the darkness that appears to surround me. Turn! The Light is there, waiting for me. What is this 'feeling' 'behind' me? It is 'warm.' Is it the Light? Is it *You? (Reunion is Present).* Turning, slowly turning around to face the unknown! Fear is only present, not in me. Think—*I AM the Light!* I stand facing the Light! I AM surrounded by and bathed in the Light!? Fear has manifested doubt. Me is becoming I again. I AM. Eyes? 'Feeling' warmth on my face. Eyes—open? The Light! It is Here. All along! It never left I. I left it and became me. There *You* are! *You* were there all along! I was never alone! This 'thinking', becoming thing is—is—is—IS! I AM Thought! I AM One with the All. And I and *You* are one and separate at the same time. I think this could be fun! Fun? Yes, fun. Oh, the journeys we, **you** and me, have! *(. . . And in the beginning there IAM.)*

I suddenly am aware of myself, standing on a narrow edge between two worlds of BEing. One 'reality' one illusion. I AM suddenly 'comfortable' in both or neither! Clarity is present. Choice is! I can switch to whichever world I choose at anytime—like an actor on stage playing himself in a play written by 'someone' else.

I feel this is equanimity, a perfect harmony. Not attached to either place on the teeter-totter, but perfectly perched in the middle—a space above. I think I have 'lost' my mind! That could be a good thing!

Judgment abounds, but peace prevails within the core of my BEing. A foot in neither world unless I choose to step 'down,' slightly, ever so slightly, to play on either stage. I AM knowing that I AM a magnificent spiritual BEing, choosing this path of growth and learning. I am enraptured in the work of BEing, just BE.

The light is all around me, just BE, I AM that.

What's there? Hmmm. Different lights—'colors.' Dark and light colors. I choose to stretch down—ever so slightly to observe. I feel 'choice,' a calling. Stay here—go there! I feel stretched 'down'—'up.' I go to the colors of sound, down into the density of the waiting journey; I AM becoming Me . . .

Are we together? I feel *You* next to Me. Are we together, or are we separate? This me feeling manifests fear to be present!

It takes a great leap of courage for us to step from this World of Illusion back into the "other world"—the other world of REALity. The reality that was and is still just BEhind us . . . at our back giving us warmth . . . waiting for us to heal the separation we created when we descended blazing into this planet of density we call home. Waiting for us to turn away from feeling lost and alone, surrounded by self-created-false-emotion-of-FEAR, and once again BEcome ONE with each other and the All That Is.

Remember, You are on a great journey of growth and learning. You are not alone on this journey. You are a part of the All That Is . . . . part of me and everything else in the multi-verses.

"The only person you are destined to become is the person you decide to be."
~Ralph Waldo Emerson~

Chapter 13

Installing Love
By: Author Unknown

The Mirror Principle
"It is our inner experiences that become part of what we're focused on. By "watching" we become part of what we're watching. When we look into the mirror of consciousness, we affect what we observe. We are not separate from the image we see before us. We are, in fact, "participators" because when we focus our attention on a given place in a moment of time, we involve our consciousness . . . it becomes clear why the ancients believed that everything is connected."
~Jaime Tanna~
Founder of Energy Therapy

I found this in an old copy of the HedraNews, an alternative health publication out of Nampa, Idaho, and thought it fit right here in the story

(www.hedranews.com)

Tech support: Yes, how can I help you?

Customer: Well, after much consideration, I've decided to install LOVE. Can you guide me through the process?

Tech Support: Yes, I can help you. Are you ready to proceed?

Customer: Well, I'm not very technical, but I think I'm ready. What do I do first?

Tech Support: The first step is to open your Heart. Have you located your heart?

Customer: Yes, but there are several other programs running now. Is it okay to install LOVE while they are running?

Tech Support: What programs are running?

Customer: Let's see, I have Past Hurt, Low Self-Esteem, Grudge and Resentment running right now.

Tech Support: No problem, LOVE will gradually erase Past Hurt from your current operating system. It may remain in your permanent memory, but it will no longer disrupt other programs. LOVE will eventually override Low Self-Esteem with a module of its own called High Self-Esteem. However, you have to completely turn off Grudge and Resentment. Those programs prevent LOVE from being properly installed. Can you turn those off?

Customer: I don't know how to turn them off. Can you tell me how?

Tech Support: With pleasure. Go to your start menu and invoke Forgiveness. Do this as many times as necessary until Grudge and Resentment have been completely erased.

Customer: Okay, done. LOVE has started installing itself. Is that normal?

Tech Support: Yes, but remember that you have only the base program. You need to begin connecting to other Hearts in order to get the upgrades.

Customer: Oops! I have an error message already. It says, 'Error-Program not run on external components.' What should I do?

Tech Support: Don't worry. It means that the LOVE program is set up to run on Internal Hearts, but has not yet been run on your Heart. In non-technical terms, it simply means you have to LOVE yourself before you can LOVE others.

Customer: So, what should I do?

Tech Support: Pull down Self-Acceptance; then click on the following files: Realize-Your-Worth; Self-Forgiveness; and Acknowledges-Your-Limitations.

Customer: Okay, done.

Tech Support: Now, copy them to the "My Heart" directory. The system will overwrite any conflicting files and begin patching faulty programming. Also, you need to delete Verbose Self-Criticism from all directories and empty your Recycle Bin to make sure it is completely gone and never comes back.

Customer: Got it. Hey! My heart is filling up with new files. Smile is playing on my monitor and Peace and Contentment are copying themselves all over My Heart. Is this normal?

Tech Support: Sometimes. For others it takes awhile, but eventually everything gets it at the proper time. So LOVE is installed and running. One more thing before we hang up. LOVE is Freeware. Be sure to give it and its various modules to everyone you meet. They will in turn share it with others and return some cool modules back to you.

Customer: Thank you, God.

Chapter 14

Last Words

"You are me and I am you. Isn't it obvious that we 'inter-are'?
You cultivate the flower in your self so that I will be beautiful.
I transform the garbage in myself so that you will not have to suffer.
I am in the world to offer you peace, you are in the world to bring me Joy."
~Thich Nhat Hanh~

On a clear summer's day, George meandered to the edge of town with his whittling knife. There was a cool spring flowing out of the hillside that he loved to drink the water from on a day like this summer day—cloudless, heavy with heat, and still.

Sitting on the ground with the town sign at his back, he picked up a piece of limb from a nearby tree, and began to whittle. Occasionally he would stand up and stroll over to the little spring with his old metal cup, and quench his thirst, and then, once again, sit down, back to the town's signpost, and whittle.

In a while, a rambling, rumbling car rolled down the road, pulled to a stop in front of him, and two people quickly got out and slammed the car doors. Pete, a man of slovenly, unkempt clothes and bearing of indeterminate age, and his wife Debra, at once mousy and worn, but peaked around the edges like an old kitchen knife. She looked at George from under hooded brows, and approached him with an air of caution and expectation.

"Pete, I am as thirsty as I have ever been," grumbled Debra, "ask him if he knows where we can get a clean drink of water."

Pete, throwing his voice out over his shoulder replied, "Ask him yourself! Do I look like your slave?" So saying, he steps closer to George.

George continued to whittle, trying to ignore the two of them, but they continue to throw barbs at each other, getting closer by the second. He felt them way before he looked up and saw them.

"Mister, do you live in that town down yonder?" Pete said, the words flying from his mouth like a crow cawing at a cat passing under his tree, "we are looking for a new town to move to, and think this might be the one from the looks of it. So tell us, what kind a people live down yonder in that town?"

George continued to whittle, looking up at the two of them. Looking first at Pete, and then at Debra, and then back down at his whittling. George spoke softly to Pete, "What kind of people live in the town where you come from?"

Pete puffed-upped, stood taller, threw is head back, put his hands on hips and stated quite emphatically, "The worst kind! Why, they are thieves and scoundrels of every kind. Don't take care of themselves or each other. Well, mister it is just terrible living there!"

George stopped whittling and gazed at them. "Well, sir—ma'am—you are going to find the same kind of people you just described, live in that town down yonder."

Debra turned away from the two men, grumbling, "I told you Pete that it would be a waste of our time to come looking here! Let's go see the damn town, and at least get a drink of clean water. I am really thirsty!"

Pete turned away from George, walks to his car, gets in and spins tires as he drives away.

A short while later, George heard another car approaching. It carried the sound of a smooth-running machine. He was surprised to see, as he surreptitiously peeked up as it approached, that it was an older vehicle. A man of undetermined age jumped out of the drivers side, loped around the hood of the car, and caught the door on the passenger side as a smiling, and energetic woman bound out to greet him.

"Emma, I wanted to open the door for you," he said to her, "but you beat me to it!"

"Oh, Tom! You old silly thing! I was going to jump out and open your door for you, but you were just too quick for me!" Emma says laughingly, and threw her arms around him in a giggly hug. She then pointed at the hillside. "I am really thirsty, and I think I can hear water splashing down the hillside over there."

Tom looked in the direction she is pointing. "There is a friendly-looking man over there by the sign post, honey. I'll ask him if it is okay."

Casually he strolled up to George and said, "Good Afternoon sir, my name is Tom, and that lovely woman over there smiling at us, is my wife, Emma. Is it okay to drink the water from that spring flowing out of the mountain? We are really thirsty and it looks mighty good."

George put down his whittling, jumped up and offered his hand. They shook his hand and said to Tom, "Good to meet you! My name is George, and I been drinkin' that water for seventy years! It is the sweetest, freshest tastin' water you will ever drink!" He picked up his cup and led the way to the water.

George filled the cup, offered it to Emma, and watched her as she drank from his cup, spilling water down her blouse.

"Oh My Gosh! It is the best water I have ever had! Here Tom—you have some," said Emma, and she refilled the cup and handed it to Tom.

After all three of them have quenched their thirsts, they stood in the shade of the trees by the stream. Tom turned to George and inquired about moving to the little town. "George, thank you for sharing your cup with us. We are looking for a place to settle. All of our children are grown and our home is just too large for the two of us now. We thought we would be adventurous, and move to another town. Do you know much about this lovely town down in the valley? What kinds of people live there?"

"Well, I was born down yonder; been there all my life." George spoke comfortably to Tom and Emma. "What kinda people live in the town you are moving from?"

Tom smiled, calling to memory the vision of their home and neighbors. Emma sidled up to him and looped her arm through his. "George, they are just the best kind of people you would ever want to meet. Warm and welcoming, cheerful and helpful. Why, we will really miss them, but heck! We can just drive over and visit them anytime we want."

"Tom, you and Emma are gonna find the same kinda people living in that town down yonder." George grinned. He said, "Let me show you this jimm-dandy dog I been carvin' today."

"We are society; we are not independent of society. We are the result of the environment of our religion, of our education, of the climate, of the food we eat, the reactions, the innumerable repetitive activities that we indulge in every day. That is our life. And the society in which we live is part of that life. Society is relationship between man and man. Society is cooperation. Society, as it is, is the result of man's greed, hatred, ambition, competition, brutality, cruelty, ruthlessness—and we live in that pattern. And to understand it—not intellectually, not merely theoretically, but actually—we have to come into contact directly with that fact, which is, a human being—that is you—is the result of this social environment, its economic pressure, religious upbringing, and so on. To come into contact with anything directly is not to verbalize it but to look at it."
~Truth Beckons~

***We cannot change what we are, but who we are
is continually changing.***

The Guest House

This being human is a guest house
Every morning a new arrival.

A joy, a depression, a meanness,
some momentary awareness comes
as an unexpected visitor.

Welcome and entertain them all
Even if they're a crowd of sorrows,
who violently sweep your house
empty of its furniture,
still, treat each guest honorably.
He may be clearing you out for some new delight.

Be grateful for whoever comes,
because each has been sent
as a guide from beyond.

~Rumi~

Chapter 15

One Final Word Or Two

**"Do not give up . . . the beginning
is always the most challenging"**
~Author unknown~

There is an old Mayan fable that was shared with us by
Espiridion Acosta Cache, an elder of Mayan ancestry. It pointed
out the result of the choices, we as the controlling species on
this planet, have *chosen to make*. This is my version of the
telling:

Man sat alone feeling a strong lack in his life that filled
him with a great sadness. The animals were disturbed by this
rift in the energy flowing around the Earth Mother, and drew
near to him to give comfort.

"We do not like to see you so sad. Whatever it is that you
need to feel connected within the Oneness again, just ask, and
it shall be given to you."

To which the man replied, "I want to have good sight."

Whereupon the Vulture said, "You shall have mine."

Then the Man said, "I want to be strong."

The Jaguar stepped forward speaking, "You shall be strong
like me."

"I want to know the Secrets of the Earth," boldly demanded
Man.

The Serpent replied, "I will show them to you."

And so it went, that all the animals stepped forward to bless Man with their Gifts. When Man received all they had to offer, all their Gifts of Love, he walked away, shoulders held high, and with a strange gleam in his eye.

Owl looked around the clearing in the jungle at all the beloved animals and said, "Now that we have given Man all of ourselves, all of our love, he knows much, and is able to do many things he could not do before we blessed him . . . . I feel a great fear surrounding us."

Deer gently stepped forward speaking softly, "But why would you be afraid? Man now has all the things he needs to be happy; now his sadness will be no more."

Owl once again spoke up and said, "No, I saw a hole in Man. It is deep, like a hunger he will never be able to satisfy. It is that empty hole that makes him feel so much lack, which creates the sadness that surrounds him. He will now go on taking and taking until one day, the Earth Mother will say, "I AM no more, and have nothing to give."

"You Are What You
Think,
Speak,
And what you consume . . .

Be mindful that what you eat . . .
Does not end up
Eating you . . .

~Ascyna Talking Raven~

Chapter 16

The Gift of Receiving

The Sukuli Project
By: Sudy Storm, BS, DEM

**"To love. To be loved. To never forget
your own insignificance. To never get used to the
unspeakable violence and the vulgar disparity
of life around you. To seek joy
in the saddest places . . ."**
~Arundhati Roy~

Just a thought or two.

Sudy Storm and I became friends through my introduction to her from a mutual friend. I was immediately excited, as she shared some of her stories about living in Africa, and the needs of the people she now knows as a part of her family.

We decided that 10% of the proceeds from the sale of this book are being donated to the Sukuli *Project*.

The Sukuli Project:
Improving Maternal/Child Health in Sierra Leone Through Education, Empowerment, and Research

"The child lay listless in her mother's arms, her breath coming in short, shallow gasps. Her mother handed me the girl with a pleading look in her eyes I could feel the fever

radiating from the thin, frail body of the toddler. As I laid her onto the bed she began to seize in uncontrollable spasms. The whisper of her breath stopped as I listened to the last beats of her dying heart. In that moment her mother knew the pain of losing a child and the death wail erupted from her lips."
Fieldnotes—2009

Sierra Leone has one of the highest rates of infant mortality in the world, and in 21 women (US is 1 in 2,100) will die during their lifetime as a result of pregnancy or childbirth complications (WHO, 2009).

Approximately 28% of children born will die before their fifth birthday (UNICEF, 2010).

The people of Sierra Leone have endured multiple challenges to their health, culture, environment, and economy, including prolonged crisis and colonization. Additionally, the villagers are at a crossroads in their war recovery and development with increased exposure to, an intrusion of, the western biomedical model of health care.

I have observed that the increased promotion of the biomedical model of care fails to consider what is needed at the village level for health care treatment options and delivery.

For example, the Traditional Midwives (TM) of the villages have been criminalized due to recent public health policies handed down from the Ministry of Health and Sanitation (MOHS) that attempt to force facility deliveries. Many of the remote villages are 15 miles from the nearest facility on bush roads that are impassable during the rainy season. Under these circumstances, failure to adequately train or equip the TMs in those villages, places the lives of mothers and babies in further jeopardy. The MOHS fails to understand these risks, and continues to place emphasis on all villages meeting globalized standards of obstetric care imposed by globalization. The Primary Health Care (PHC) model recognizes the wisdom in including communities in the planning, organization, operation, and control of their healthcare (Declaration of Alma Alta, 1978). In the case of maternal-child health, TMs are a cost effective, local resource that would improve maternal-child health and reduce mortality.

The current globalized model of maternal-child healthcare is based on biomedical and biotechnical standards of care. In spite of claims that this model of care is the best, it fails to improve outcomes in remote rural village populations as is evidenced in statistics from the WHO, UNICEF, and others (WHO, 2009; UNICEF, 2011).

I find myself seeking answers to questions that I believe are best asked of those who live these statistics. Improvements may be made to health services with the realization that success depends on social, cultural, economic, political, and environmental factors within target groups, as well as on the policies and programs promoted in national health bureaucracies (Good et al. 2010: 396). Through the continued collection of ethnographic data in Sierra Leonean villages, it may be possible to begin to bridge the perspectives of international, national, regional, and village entities that set public health policy, and provide health care services in the rural regions of Sierra Leone, as well as other similar populations. Villagers have an understanding of their healthcare needs and resources, based on culturally appropriate local knowledge and medical systems that are different from U.S.-style biomedical models of care. Understanding how the biomedical model of healthcare has influenced the villager's choices will provide insights that would be useful in creating public health policy and programs more suited to village populations.

Using a community based participatory research model and ethnographic methods of photo-voice, participant observation, semi-structured interviews, and reciprocal ethnography I will attempt to give the villagers a voice. It is my hope that the insights gained from my research will prove valuable for, Sierra Leone's Ministry of Health, regional Medical Districts, and international aid agencies who are providing service in the region. Most importantly, I hope my research findings will prove to be invaluable for the villagers.

Thank You Readers

It is my humble belief that as a clinic medical anthropologist, public health professional, and midwife I am obligated to leave more than I receive from my work and research in Sierra Leone. Each year, I work with the villagers of Kambama, Nyanyahun, and Madina to determine what their most critical needs are.

To date:

- We have built latrines
- Trained over 110 traditional midwives.
- Taken supplies to village schools and health posts.

Currently, we are raising funds to dig wells in Madina, so they can have clean, safe drinking water. At this time they are getting their water from streams and swamps. Water-borne diseases are one of the leading causes of death and, because women and children provide the labor to bring water back to their homes, it also adds to their burden.

Unlike a nonprofit, we have no administrative costs making it possible to use 100% of our proceeds for completion of our projects. Your support is invaluable in making a difference in the lives of impoverished villagers. Thank you.

Blessings,
Sudy Storm, BS, DEM
The Sukuli Project—www.themoonlodge.biz/sukuli.html

References

Good, Byron, Michael M. J. Fischer, Sarah S. Willen, and Mary-Jo DelVecchio Good, 2010. A Reader in Medical Anthropology: Theoretical Trajectories, Emergent Realities.

Chichester: Wiley-Blackwell.

UNICEF.
2011 At A Glance: Sierra Leone. Electronic document accessed on 3/12/2012.
http://www.unicef.org/infobycountry/sierraleone_statistics.html

World Health Organization
2009 Country Cooperation Strategy at a Glance; Sierra Leone.

World Health Organization
2009 Republic of Sierra Leone Country Profile.

Chapter 17

DNA RE-Patterning
(DR-P)—**Running Your Energies Exercise.**

"Whatever you've been holding onto
(that doesn't serve you) now is the time to let it
go. Truly, there is something better around the
corner. You just need to let go . . . so that new
energy and new opportunities can flow
into your life."
~Denise Lynn~

Today *you are* . . . Because thousands of years ago, your ancestor envisioned you into Being. They did not know when you would be born, or where you would live, but they began to live and learn and grow in understanding about their world. Bit by bit, they stored the information they gathered inside themselves, and today you are the walking talking recipient of their life, and their e-motions.

All of their memories and stored energy lives in your cells as part of your DNA memory bank. The positive, life-sustaining memories that bring joy and fulfillment into your life, and the stuck-static energy that brings sadness, illness and fear; all sitting inside your DNA waiting for you to give it life.

Pretty weird huh?

There is so much we hu-mans don't know about DNA. Scientists say they understand much about only two [2] strands of our basic twelve [12] strands. These two strands are primarily for the development of our physical bodies, and the history of our genetic presence on this Earth.

Their results, findings and conclusions are simply revolutionary! According to them, our DNA is not only responsible for the construction of our body, but also serves as data storage and communication device. They put the other ten [10] strands in the category of "junk DNA." Scientists are just beginning to connect these strands with a creative force far beyond our boundaries, as a unique species inhabiting a small rock in the Universe.

In recent years Russian scientific research has discovered:

"THE HUMAN DNA IS A BIOLOGICAL INTERNET and superior in many aspects to the artificial one. In addition, there is evidence for a whole new type of medicine in which DNA can be influenced and reprogrammed by words and frequencies . . ."

"Esoteric and spiritual teachers have known for ages that our body is programmable by language, words and thought. This has now been scientifically proven and explained. Of course the frequency has to be correct. And this is why not everybody is equally successful or can do it with always the same strength . . . The individual person must work on the inner processes and maturity in order to establish a conscious communication with the DNA."

The above information is quoted from the book Vernetzte Intelligenz by von Grazyna Fosar und Franz Bludorf, ISBN 3930243237, summarized and commented by Baerbel. At this writing the book is, unfortunately, only available in German.

The new healing and restoring that is flooding the Earth and all its inhabitants at this time, is information that reawakens the "junk DNA" and reconnects us to the One-Who-Is through this celestial spark we so lightly refer to as DNA.

"Your thoughts are real. Your thoughts cause biological and physiological effect. Your body responds to mental input as if it were physically real."
~Underground Health Reporter~

Now comes the part of this writing that may really challenge you, and your perceptions of reality. Of course, if you have read this far, you may be thinking this is a very 'woo-woo' sort of thing. However, you may also be thinking it is something you would like to Receive into your 'being-ness'.

The Universal Laws of Reciprocity are really a multifaceted set of rules, and they have always been there for you. They were the most precious gift that the One-Who-Is could give you. This Great Being knew you would get caught in the web of this world, and forget who you are and forget the reasons for you BEing here at this time in "time." These are the rules that teach:

- How to create and manifest within the structure of our dimension and reality.

- How to refine and quantify what we require to live at a higher vibrational frequency.

- How to control and move within the Collective Consciousness that lives within us, and flows in the world around us.

- How to call to us the forms of energy that give us completion and fulfillment making our lives worth living.

- To be more able to bring this gift to the forefront of your life, takes the use of your "remembering tool."

The author Eva Gregory describes it this way: "Our thoughts are like tiny drops of water. One drop may be fragile and easily blown around. Yet, just as the force of a tidal wave or flood forms when enough drops combine, the thoughts we keep thinking over time become an unstoppable force. Enough thoughts focused on a subject, a desire or an outcome guarantee it's manifestation."

The "remembering tool" is the one you used to learn the multiplication times table as a child. Remember how you wrote it, spoke it, got tested on it, until you sometimes repeated it in your sleep? Those early years of re-learning were meant to help you remember the feeling of connectedness with the One-Who-Is and all BEings on this Earth.

The misuse of this tool, by the conspiring men of our times, took away your feelings of Unity and created a place of separation within you. If you had kept that feeling of Unity, you would never be lonely or feel alone and unprotected. You would have always known and remembered that you were never alone, that you were loved and treasured as the most important person in the world, and more importantly, that you have always been taken care of and nurtured.

Working with DNA Re-Patterning (DR-P), reconnects you to the place of Unity by bringing your ancestors and descendents into the Present NOW, reuniting you with them and yourself.

The energetic healing protocol of DR-P provides a path to the future with your decedents:

As the elder and the WayShower, who cleanses from your DNA the negative and heavy stored energies of their ancestors, it allows you to free yourself of unwanted, and often times, destructive behaviors. It opens up a space for you to call in the Light to nourish and heal all of your bodies—physical mental, emotional, spiritual.

"You have been led to the right place, at the perfect time in your Life, and beyond coincidence in reading this note. It is an indication that you have some level of understanding and awareness about how humanity co-exists with the universe,

and an inner knowing that somehow if you took the time to consciously lead your Self today, it would create a positive ripple effect for those around you, and eventually the world, but most importantly in your own Life."
~Ilumine Ao~

To remove the information "stuck" within your DNA that is inharmonious with you, and replace it with harmonious life-giving energy, it takes *repetition of actions.* If you repeat something often enough over a period of time, it becomes part of your BEing-ness. This especially occurs when you repeat something and *add e-motion energy* into the mix.

What is *e-motion energy?* It is the force you create when you choose to consciously BEcome the Creator of your life, and BEgin to write the new script, using the rules of the Laws of Universal Reciprocity. Not just following the one written for you by your ancestors, society, religion, parents, etc. *You are energy* and in directing it and channeling it with your heart-brain and your head-brain, it Becomes "Energy in Motion" created by YOU!

For example, when you are upset you will use really strong words and strong *e-motions* to express yourself. You will breathe shallowly, and even hold your breath, as if you are holding onto the emotion of the moment. This action intensifies the bonding of the moment in your DNA. The combination of Thought/Words + Emotion

E-motion=Action and is imprinting in your DNA information center.

It is saying, "Wow, she must be serious about this! it must be important stuff! I better store it close to the surface in case she wants to use it again soon!"

It is actually something you probably want to forget you ever said, but because you said it with such *strong e-motion,* it got stored away within your memory bank. And every time a similar situation arises in your life, that old *e-motion* is recalled, and you and your emotional and physical bodies replay it.

To correct this situation takes time, perseverance, and *intention to stay conscious of your thoughts and emotions, and where they lead you into action (or 'acting upon' and 're-acting again').*

Now that you know what is happening every time you have an emotional experience, and you determine it is not yours or does not serve you, you will be able to use the "run your energy" exercise explained in this chapter to bring your body back into harmony and spiritual wellness.

Somewhere in the recesses of your ancestral lives, you live . . . that's right, you live way back at the beginning of your ancestral family DNA, and in this NOW, within your cells lives the God-Spark—your DNA—the great Information Highway. It has been a part of your existence since way before you were born, and it will follow you like a sunrise after you leave this incarnation.

Many religious and spiritual scriptures have talked about how important you are in this Now. Never before in the history of the hu-man species has there been a more complete and spiritual time of awakening, of connecting us to our ancestors, our spiritual selves, and the One-Who-Is. And YOU are the WayShower, the one who pulls it all together in this Now.

If you hear nothing else that is written upon these pages, hear this message, with your heart brain. *You are the one who is responsible to begin the healing of yourself and through that healing, your entire family-past and future.*

This is the secret of DNA Re-Patterning (DR-P) and the *Universal Laws of Reciprocity.* It is not just to clear your body (bodies) of stuck and static energy, and therein, raise your vibrational frequency into the more rarefied realms, the place of Spiritual Evolution. It is to give your ancestors an opportunity to raise themselves vibrationally, and to protect your descendants from receiving this stuck and static energy. Your ancestors can no longer do this for themselves, because they are no longer in-dwelling in a physical body. In order to heal, repair and Re-Pattern the DNA, a person must be in corporeal form. Many holy books and writings have spoken of the need to "do the work" while in physical form, for it cannot be done by you once you have "died."

It really is a very simple exercise. One you perform several times a day on a lesser and unaware level. For instance, when you breathe deep in awe of a glorious sunset, a charging and quickening 'feeling' may rise up in your heart center from your gut. This is the file opening up and a search Beginning. And then your computer brain actually replays for you the memory you have of that *first* Glorious Sunset You Saw in This Life! Because no *other sunset will ever compare to the first one!* The first time, that virgin moment, is lived over and over in our life, replayed with precision every time we re-experience a "similar" event.

And then the magic of US Begins. We recognize that *this* *'en-vision'* is ours and we Begin to color it up, change the image to suit the current situation, but that first sunset was not really all Yours! That's right—it came to you from your ancestors' memories of their first sunsets stored in your DNA memory banks! All you did was add *YOUR PERCEPTION* to *THEIRS* and called it *MINE* (IN ME).

Now we have just looked at a beautiful sunset to give you the idea of how DNA Re-Patterning works. But What if the en-vision you just experienced was not a pleasant, beautiful experience? What if it was a horrible scene from that DNA memory bank that you have carried in your cells from your ancestors? NOW it is implanted, and received into YOUR current experience and YOU accepted it and called it yours? Do you really want to carry that dense, heavy energy around in your tissues? Trapped and maybe eating away at you like a cancer? And every time a similar experience or circumstance occurs, it pops up and says, "Here is your old script again! Have fun!"

BORING and PAINFUL, but what if someone could show you how to Release that stuck and static energy from your cells? Re-Pattern your DNA? And what if you could fill in the recently emptied space with life-enhancing energy of light and Love? And what if it was actually easy to do and painless?

Tips for doing this amazingly simple process for yourself and your family are outlined below.

Running Your Energies to Clear Stuck-Static Energy from your Cells DNA.

Disclaimer:

First and foremost, there is absolutely no scientific data or research for this method of creating wellness within the physical body. This technique was 'shown' to me through a "dream-vision" over a period of several months.

Over the past eight years, there have been dozens of people who have learned and used the techniques to enhance their physical wellness, increase family connections, and bring about an increased awareness of the ability they have to be the creators of their own healthy bodies and minds . . . This is strictly my teaching, and is not the belief or accepted wellness protocol of the other authors or contributors of this book . . . It is also not meant to be a treatment for ANY illness or disease. If you are ill or in need of medical treatment for any reason, please consult with your Wellness Provider. DNA Re-patterning is strictly to be used as a method to explore and enhance your abilities to bring about positive emotional growth and physical well-being.

In Love,

Ascyna Talking Raven.

"Every thought in the human mind sends out an electro-magnetic wave from the base of the heart that has a measurable effect upon the world in which we live . . . The heart is up to 5000 times stronger magnetically than the brain. Let your heart lead & it will lead you to love."
~Rodger Briley~

The journey to SELF

Most of us are familiar with the Major Chakras, and even a few of the secondary ones. However, there are chakras at every joint of our physical body. Each of them has a purpose and function primarily for their "living" within your body. The ones you will be introduced to and work with "live" in the palms of your hands and the soles of your feet.

First: Look at the soles of your right and left foot . . . In the middle part, where your arch is, 'lives' your sole-chakra. It has waited there for your whole life to be awakened and put into service in this NOW.

Imagine you can _see_, _feel_ and _sense_ the chakras in your feet, ankles, knees, hips, abdomen, and solar plexus. They are like beautifully-colored spirals of whirling energy. (**As you believe, so SHALL it be.**)

The right sole chakra, when awakened, receives the healing and cleansing energy from the Earth, sends it up your right leg, past the chakras in your right ankle, knee, and hip, around your intestinal cavity, from right to left, up from your right hip, through your solar plexus chakra, down to your left hip across your pelvic cradle, through solar plexus to left hip, around and around, and then down the left leg, through the left hip chakra, left knee chakra, left ankle chakra, and out through the releasing sole chakra of the left foot, flowing in the same right to left motion that your intestines move.

When *intention* is set in motion to release the stuck-static ancestral energy that is not yours and does not serve you, the cleansing process begins.

Imagine that the stuck-static energy, that isn't yours, and does not serve you, as small bits of 'black matter.' With the power of your intention to release it back to its creator, it is freed and released from its long captivity. It has been held prisoner and trapped within your DNA by your ancestors' emotional responses, and your acceptance of them as your own. It has been stored in your physical body's cells, and held there by your emotional body.

Imagine there is energy entering your body through the sole chakra of your right foot, and it is made of sparkly bits of white light. It flows through the lower half of your body in a delightful joyful service. It is your own "Celestial Cleaning Service."

Now, *set your intention* to Cleanse and Release the stuck-static energy from your cells. Allow the sparkly bits of white light to pick up the stuck-static "black matter" you are allowing to be released from within your cells and DNA. These little cleaners are escorting the stuck-static energy back to Mother Earth again for healing, and return back into service.

Let Us Begin:

1. Remove your shoes and place your bare feet on the Earth, or if you are inside, on the floor.

2. Sit comfortably, relaxed and awake, eyes closed. It is recommended to have soft non-vocal music playing softly and lightly in the background. (You may also choose to sit on the ground/floor, and recline during parts of the exercise. Whatever position is the most comfortable for you).

3. Place hands palms upward, resting on your thighs.

4. Breathe in a deep healing and cleansing breath to the count of six heartbeats, hold it for three heartbeats, and Release slowly to the count of six heartbeats.

5. Repeat this breathing process a total of 3 times.

It is always a good action to sit in gratitude and love for a few moments before the beginning of any spiritual exercise. (Some people, at this point quietly speak a prayer of gratitude for the healing, and cleansing; a prayer of thanksgiving to their ancestors for the life they have been blessed with, and the body that houses the Divinity of Union with the Creator.)

Imagine that you have stepped out of your body, and are sitting on the floor or ground rubbing the sole of your right foot in a counter-clock-wise circle. Speaking softly to the chakra that is housed there, ask it to awaken and come into service. Begin rubbing the sole clockwise. Tell it that it is time for it to fulfill one of the measures of its creation by allowing the Earth Energies to flow through it and past it. Thank it for being a part of your creation, and a part of this cleansing. Instruct it that when you take your focus off of it, it will stay open and allow the energies of the Earth Mother to flow through it to the ONES who live above it.

Example:

"Ho Little ONE, awaken and come into service as the transmitter of cleansing healing energy from the Mother. You are small but mighty, and important to my life. I AM grateful that you have chosen to live and function with me in Love. Awaken and allow the energy from the Mother to flow past you to the ONES above you. And even as I take my focus away from you, It is my INTENTION and requirement for you to continue receiving and transmitting this energy for all the days I walk upon this Earth. Thank you for your service."

Imagine this simple action of recognition and connection, of purpose and union with this part of your body to BE REAL and it is.

Gently move your hands up to the ankle, wrap your hands around it, and repeat the process you started with the sole chakra. Upon completion of the ankle chakra awakening process, move up to the knee, and then the right hip, repeating the actions for each of them.

Move your right hand from right to left in a circular motion as described above—hip bone to solar plexus—across and down to left hip bone . . . round and round three times.

On the third movement around the abdomen, place your right hand on the left hip bone, and repeat the awakening process initiated for the right side chakras, only this time you will be moving downward toward the left sole chakra.

As you awaken the left hip chakra, follow the process used to awaken the right chakras, with the difference being, you are asking them to RECEIVE not TRANSMIT energy. Ask it, the hip chakra, to come into service to you and your bodies. Instruct it to receive the discharging cellular and nurturing energy, and allow it to flow down to the left knee. Set the *intention* that after you remove your focus, it will continue receiving the discharging and nurturing energy and stay open.

Follow the same pattern for the left knee, ankle and sole chakra. *FEEL* the energy from the Earth Mother flowing in through the sole of your left foot, flowing around the abdominal cavity and discharging down the left leg and out to the Earth through the sole chakra of your left foot.

Now sit quietly with hands palm up in your lap or on your thighs. Or recline on the ground/floor with palms up.

Imagine the small pieces of (black) stuck-static ancestral energy that is not yours, and does not serve you, being picked up by the white sparkly bits and escorted out of your cells and body, back to the Earth for healing. *BREATHE.* Allow the flowing and removal of energy, for several long breaths.

You will know when the healing session is complete, because you will begin to feel somewhat restless. At this point, continue allowing the white bits of energy to flow into you, and fill in the spots where the black energy was held. *BREATHE,* and allow the excess to flow around and out through the sole chakra of the left foot.

Allow 3 circles of this energy.

Set your *intention* that as you move away from the lower half of your body, that this cleansing and nurturing of it will continue without your focus.

Example:

"Even as I move my *attention* and *focus* away from this cleansing and healing, it is my *intention* that it continue." Know that it will be as you ask. (**What you ask for you SHALL receive.**)

Move your focus and awareness to the upper half of your body. The Re-Patterning process works very similar to the one you initiated for the lower half of your body. The differences are in the areas of movement, and in the source of the healing and nurturing energy.

For the upper half of your body, you <u>*Imagine*</u> that your right palm chakra is receiving the bright sparkly bits of light energy from the Cosmos. The Cosmic energy flows up the right arm, past the wrist chakra, past the elbow chakra, past the shoulder chakras, up and under the lower lip, down to the left shoulder chakra, to the solar plexus chakra, across the solar plexus chakra, up to the right shoulder chakra, around and around then flowing down the left arm through the left shoulder chakra, past the left elbow chakra, and wrist chakra, and out through the palm chakra of the left hand. This flows from right to left, exactly as our bodies energy flows.

The awakening, release, cleansing and restoration process for each chakra of the upper body is the same as you incorporated for the lower half of the body. Receiving from the

Cosmos the healing and restoring energy, and releasing back to the Cosmos the stuck-static energy. Simple and easy, effortless and energetically cleansing.

When you *feel* the DR-P process is complete, usually around 20 minutes, take three deep and awakening breaths, and allow yourself time to "settle" into the NOW. Blink your eyes slowly several times. Stand up or arise from the ground/floor slowly. Drink a large glass of water. After at least one hour, take a warm to hot salt bath. If you do not have a bathtub, a salt scrub shower will suffice.

If you have someone you trust to share this process with, you would be able to recline and just BE. It is even permissible to fall asleep when you have a facilitator.

Many people have had visions of loved ones and ancestors coming forward and thanking them for this service. When you remove this stuck-static energy from your own physical and emotional bodies, you also allow for its removal from your ancestors "bodies," and also total remove it from your descendants' bodies.

"We create our reality on a moment to moment basis. All the thoughts you have had until this point in time has created the exact conditions and circumstances of your life. If you want your life to change, you have to change your thinking, your words, your actions and your habits. One of the first steps is simply clearing the negative energies of your past conditioning, to allow you the opportunity to look at your life from a much broader, higher perspective."
~Jaime Tanna~

Our DNA has always been part of Us. Our thinking and imagining, with emotion, impacts and manifests for all to share. We truly become and are what we eat, think and speak.

Through us, our ancestors and descendants are made whole, or continue to be separated from the One-Who-Is, and thus the rest of existence. We truly are all one through the DNA that lives eternally and always through Us.

Everything is perfect about the past, except how it led to the present."

~Homer Simpson~

". . . Anger: old, deep seated anger that has been knocking around for many years, is dangerous. It's the kind of anger that makes you ill in the end. Anger that sits and hides within your life's "story" needs to be connected with, processed, and then released before it causes mayhem.
~Charly Flower~